The Troubadour of Knowledge

Studies in Literature and Science

published in association with the
Society for Literature and Science

Titles in the series

Transgressive Readings: The Texts of Franz Kafka and Max Planck
by Valerie D. Greenberg

A Blessed Rage for Order: Deconstructionism, Evolution, and Chaos
by Alexander J. Argyros

Of Two Minds: Hypertext Pedagogy and Poetics
by Michael Joyce

The Artificial Paradise: Science Fiction and American Reality
by Sharona Ben-Tov

Conversations on Science, Culture, and Time
by Michel Serres with Bruno Latour

Genesis by Michel Serres

The Natural Contract by Michel Serres

Dora Marsden and Early Modernism: Gender, Individualism, Science
by Bruce Clarke

The Meaning of Consciousness by Andrew Lohrey

The Troubadour of Knowledge by Michel Serres

MICHEL SERRES

The Troubadour of Knowledge

Translated by Sheila Faria Glaser
with William Paulson

Ann Arbor

THE UNIVERSITY OF MICHIGAN PRESS

English translation copyright © by the University of Michigan 1997
Originally published in French as *Le Tiers-Instruit*
© by François Bourin 1991
All rights reserved
Published in the United States of America by
The University of Michigan Press
Manufactured in the United States of America
⊛ Printed on acid-free paper

2000   1999   1998   1997   4   3   2   1

A CIP catalog record for this book is available from the British Library.

Library of Congress Cataloging-in-Publication Data

Serres, Michel.
    [Tiers-instruit.   English]
    The troubadour of knowledge / Michel Serres : translated by Sheila
Faria Glaser, with William Paulson.
        p.   cm. — (Studies in literature and science)
    ISBN 0-472-09551-X. — ISBN 0-472-06551-3 (pbk.)
    I. Title.   II. Series.
PQ2679.E679T5313   1997
194—dc21   97-8493
                                                                      CIP

The publisher is grateful for a partial subvention for translation
from the French Ministry of Culture.

For Anne-Marie,
Emmanuelle, and Stéphanie

Philomuthos, philosophos pôs.
Philosophos, philomuthos pôs.

ARISTOTLE

Translators' Note

The French title of this book, "Le Tiers-Instruit"—literally, "the third-instructed (one)" or "the instructed third"—parallels, in French, such well-known expressions as "third estate," "third world," and "excluded third." It refers, then, to the subject of a third kind of instruction outside the dominant first two: outside scientific and literary education, or the natural and human sciences. In the text, we have generally translated this phrase literally. "The Third-Instructed," however, would have made an unappealing and perplexing book title. "The Troubadour of Knowledge" was chosen to reflect Michel Serres's identification of the third-instructed with the figure of the troubadour, his equation of learning and knowing with finding and inventing. Throughout the text, knowledge, learning, and philosophy are linked to travel, to seeking and encountering, to the intersection of genres and disciplines, and to the felicitous use of language. The connection to the poet-musicians who traveled through medieval Provence is made explicit in the second part of the book in the section entitled "Another Name for the Third-Instructed: Troubadour."

Contents

Preface

Secularism

Back from the inspection of his lunar lands, Harlequin, emperor, appears on stage, for a press conference. What marvels did he see in traversing such extraordinary places? The public is hoping for wonderous eccentricities.

"No, no," he responds to the questions that are fired at him, "everywhere everything is just as it is here, identical in every way to what one can see ordinarily on the terraqueous globe. Except that the degrees of grandeur and beauty change."

Disappointed, the audience cannot believe its ears: elsewhere must surely be different. Was he incapable of observing anything in the course of his voyage? At first silent, dumbfounded, they begin to stir once Harlequin pedantically repeats his lesson: nothing new under the sun or on the moon. The word of King Solomon precedes that of the satellite potentate. There is nothing more to be said, no need for commentary.

Whether royal or imperial, whoever wields power, in fact, never encounters in space anything other than obedience to his power, thus his law: power does not move. When it does, it strides on a red carpet. Thus reason never discovers, beneath its feet, anything but its own rule.

Haughtily, Harlequin looks the spectators up and down with ridiculous disdain and arrogance.

From the middle of the class, which is becoming unruly, a true and troublesome wit rises and extends his hand to designate the Harlequin's cape.

"Hey!" he cries, "You who say that everywhere everything is just as it is here, can you also make us believe that your cape is the same in every part, for example in front as it is on the back?"

Shocked, the public no longer knows whether to be silent or to laugh; and, in fact, the king's clothing announces the opposite of what he claims. A motley composite made of pieces, of rags or scraps of every size, in a thousand forms and different colors, of varying ages, from different sources, badly basted, inharmoniously juxtaposed, with no attention paid to proximity, mended according to circumstance, according to need, accident, and contingency—does it show a kind of world map, a map of the comedian's travels, like a suitcase studded with stickers? Elsewhere, then, is never like here, no part resembles any other, no province could be compared to this or that one, and all cultures are different. The map-cum-greatcoat belies what the king of the moon claims.

Gaze with all your eyes at this landscape—zebrine, tigroid, iridescent, shimmering, embroidered, distressed, lashed, lacunar, spotted like an ocelot, colorfully patterned, torn up, knotted together, with overlapping threads, worn fringe, everywhere unexpected, miserable, glorious, so magnificent it takes your breath away and sets your heart beating.

Powerful and flat, speech, monotonous, reigns and vitrifies space; superb in its misery, this improbable garment dazzles. The derisory emperor, who chatters like a parrot, is enveloped in a world map of badly bracketed multiplicities. Pure and simple language or a composite and badly matched garment, glistening, beautiful like a thing: which to choose?

"Are you dressed in the road map of your travels?" says the perfidious wit.

Everyone titters. The king is caught out and discomfited.

Harlequin quickly figured out the only escape from the ridicule his position invites: all he can do is to take off the coat that belies him. He gets up, hesitating, looks, gaping, at the panels of his outfit, then, devoutly, looks at his public, then looks again at his coat, as if seized with embarrassment. The audience laughs, a bit foolishly. He takes his time, everyone waits. The Emperor of the Moon finally makes up his mind.

Harlequin gets undressed; after much grimacing and graceless contortion, he finally lets the motley coat drop to his feet.

Another iridescent envelope then appears: he was wearing another rag beneath the first veil. Disconcerted, the audience laughs again. Thus it is necessary to start again, because the second envelope, similar to the coat, is composed of new pieces and old bits. It's impossible to describe the second tunic without repeating, like a litany, tigroid, iridescent, zebrine, studded.

Harlequin keeps getting undressed. Another shimmering dress, a new embroidered tunic, then a kind of striated veil appear successively, and still another colorfully patterned body stocking spotted like an ocelot . . . The audience guffaws, increasingly stupefied; Harlequin never gets to his last outfit, while the one before last resembles the antepenultimate as closely as could be desired: motley, composite, torn up . . . Harlequin is wearing a thick layer of these harlequin coats.

Indefinitely, the naked retreats beneath the masks and the living beneath the doll or the statue swollen with bits of cloth. Certainly, the first coat makes the juxtaposition of pieces visible, but the multiplicity, the overlap of successive, implied envelopes shows and also conceals it. Onion, artichoke, the Harlequin never ceases to shed his layers or to peel off his knotted capes; the public never stops laughing.

All of a sudden, silence; seriousness, even gravity, descends on the audience—the king is naked. Discarded, the last screen has just fallen.

Stupefaction! Tattooed, the Emperor of the Moon exhibits a colorfully patterned skin, more a medley of colors than skin. His whole body looks like a fingerprint. Like a painting on a curtain, the tattooing—striated, iridescent, embroidered, damasked, shimmering—is an obstacle to looking, as much as the clothing or the coats that fall to the ground.

Let the last veil fall and the secret be revealed; it is as complicated as all the barriers that protected it. Even the Harlequin's skin belies the unity presumed in what he says, because it, too, is a harlequin's coat.

The audience tries to laugh again, but it can't anymore: perhaps the man should strip himself—whistles, jeers. Can someone be asked to skin himself?

The audience has seen, it holds its breath, you could hear a pin drop. The Harlequin is only an emperor, even a derisory one, the Harlequin is only a Harlequin, multiple and diverse, undulating and plural, when he dresses and gets undressed: thus named and titled because he protects himself, defends himself, and hides, multiply, indefinitely. Suddenly, the spectators, as a whole, have managed to see right through the whole mystery.

Here he is now unveiled, and delivered, defenseless, to intuition. Harlequin is a hermaphrodite, a mixed body, male and female. Scandalized, the audience is moved to the point of tears. The naked androgyne mixes genders so that it is impossible to locate the vicinities, the places, or borders where the sexes stop and begin: a man lost in a female, a female mixed with a male. This is how he or she shows him/herself: as a monster.

Monster? A sphinx, beast and girl; centaur, male and horse; unicorn, chimera, composite and mixed body; where and how to locate the site of suture or of blending, the groove where the bond is knotted and tightens, the scar where the lips, the right and the left, the high and the low, but also the angel and the beast, the vain, modest, or vengeful victor and the humble or repugnant victim, the inert and the living, the miserable and the very rich, the complete idiot and the vivacious fool, the genius and the imbecile, the master and the slave, the emperor and the clown are joined? A monster certainly, but normal. What shadow must be cast aside, now, in order to reveal the point of juncture?

Harlequin-Hermaphrodite uses both hands; he is not ambidextrous but a completed left-hander. You could see this clearly; when he undressed, his capes twirling on both sides, he was adroit even on the left. The charms of childhood combined with the wrinkles proper to the old made one wonder about his age: adolescent or dotard? But above all, when the skin and flesh appeared, the whole world discovered his mixed origin: mulatto, half-caste, Eurasian, hybrid in general, and on what grounds? Quadroon, octoroon? And if he was not playing the king, even as comedy, one would have the urge to say bastard or mongrel, crossbreed. Mixed blood, mestizo or mestiza, diluted.

What could the current, tattooed, ambidextrous monster, hermaphrodite and half-breed, make us see now under his skin? Yes, flesh and blood. Science speaks of organs, functions, cells, and molecules, to admit finally that it's been a long time since life has been spoken of in laboratories, but it never says flesh, which, very precisely, designates the mixture of muscles and blood, skin and hairs, bones, nerves, and diverse functions, which thus mixes what the relevant disciplines analyze. Life throws the dice or plays cards. Harlequin discovers, in the end, his flesh. Combined, the mixed flesh and blood of the Harlequin are still quite likely to be taken for a harlequin coat.

Quite some time ago, a number of spectators left the room, tired of failed dramatic moments, irritated with this turn from comedy to tragedy, having come to laugh and been disappointed at having to think. Some, doubtless specialists in their field, had even understood, on their own, that each portion of their knowledge also looks like Harlequin's coat, because each works at the intersection or the interference of many other disciplines and, sometimes, of almost all of them. In this way, their academy or the encyclopedia formally joined commedia dell'arte.

Now then, when everybody had his back turned, and the oil lamps were giving signs of flickering out, and it seemed that this evening the improvisation had ended up being a flop, someone suddenly called out, as if something new were playing in a place where everything had, that evening, been a repetition, so that the public as a whole, turned back as one, all looking toward the stage, violently illuminated by the dying fires of the footlights:

"Pierrot! Pierrot!" the audience cried, "*Pierrot Lunaire!*"

In the very same spot where the Emperor of the Moon had stood was a dazzling, incandescent mass, more clear than pale, more transparent than wan, lilylike, snowy, candid, pure and virginal, all white.

"Pierrot! Pierrot!" cried the fools again as the curtain fell.

As they filed out, they were asking:

"How can the thousand hues of an odd medley of colors be reduced to their white summation?"

"Just as the body," the learned responded, "assimilates and retains the various differences experienced during travel and returns home a half-breed of new gestures and other customs, dissolved in the body's attitudes and functions, to the point that it believes that as far as it is concerned nothing has changed, so the secular miracle of tolerance, of benevolent neutrality welcomes, in peace, just as many apprenticeships in order to make the liberty of invention, thus of thought, spring forth from them."

Upbringing

Envoi

Thank you. My heart-felt gratitude goes first to the late schoolmaster, whose face, voice, and hands will remain in my memory until death and who, several decades ago, made of me what the right-handed majority compassionately call a thwarted left-hander, but which I have to describe joyously as a completed half. No other event sculpted my body with greater consequences, no one decided direction/meaning for me in a more revolutionary way.

For once, the teaching body, which gets up to speak and convince, or leans over to write, presents itself to its public in its naked naïveté: like an organism, giving rise to language and thought certainly, but first of all carnally modeled by an anonymous teacher whom I thank.

Body

No one doubts the wisdom of the reform that allowed left-handed people, my fellow creatures, to write their own way. To thwart them would have cast them into a vague population of stammerers, perverts, or neurotics, or so the theory goes. In principle, I am part of that sickly group to which today I give voice and which I represent. Strange tidings: all is for the best in the best of all possible bodies.

How can a right-handed person be described? As a severed organism, suffering from severe hemiplegia. The pen, the knife, the hammer, and the racket are gathered together in one hand, while the other carries nothing. Hot and supple, one side of the body and its extension lives, trailing behind it a sort of cadaverous twin, stiff and cold, contemptible and impotent—in short, unconscious.

That is only half the truth. How, in turn, can one describe a left-handed person? As an organism traversed by a crevice, paraplegic, sick. Pencil, fork, ball, and scissors fit only his one hand, whereas the second hangs, sleeps. Alert, sweet, present, here is one side of space and of life, while the half-body pushes or drags, with no chance of striking a balance, a hard, absent, dead double, a weight without strength, an unconscious mass with no language.

All things considered, then, one is the same as the other. Each, divorced, is composed of two twins of which only one, whichever side you choose, has the right to life, the second never having been born. Thus, to allow the left-hander to remain so amounts to creating right-handed people; other right-handed people, from the other side. The liberation of the left now looks to me like a right-wing decision.

Hemiplegic bodies have granted each other recognition and force everyone to remain in the stupid pathology of division.

No, we are not one, but two. Is each person's body, left-hander or right-hander, composed of two enemy brothers, perfect twins, albeit enantiomorphs, that is to say, at once symmetrical and asymmetrical, competing and thwarted twins, one of whom has always already killed the other, whose cadaver he wears, strapped to his back, just as the generals of ancient Rome dragged vanquished and enslaved adversaries behind them in triumph? Does the use, which certain ethnographers have found to be universal, of only the right side of the body derive from immemorial practices of sacrifice? The right-hander or left-hander can never stand to have the other at his side, unless he is dead or stillborn.

I preach against the death penalty in this matter, in favor of the reconciled body, of friendship between brothers, in favor, finally, of that rare tolerance, or maybe love, that takes pleasure in the other, his closest neighbor, living happily— who, in order to do so, at least had the chance or the right to be born.

The brain is divided into two halves, each of which through crossed fasciculi, communicate with the other side of the body, respectively. Hemiplegia paralyzes both the left side of the body and the right side of the brain or the left side of the brain and the right side of the body. It seems to me that it is better to live, speak, or think with all one's organs than to cut a dark half out of the whole. No one holds this principle in esteem, despite its beautiful, harmonious, and total self-evidence: how to explain humanity's passion, seemingly that of all humanity, for an illness that forces our half-body to be stuck to a cadaver, as in a hideous marriage?

Therefore, thanks first of all to the one who trained me in the plenitude and saturation proper to a complete body.

Nothing gives greater direction than to change direction. I recount through images the memory of my mutation.

No one really knows how to swim until he has crossed a large and impetuous river or a rough strait, an arm of the sea, alone. In a pool there is only the ground—a territory for a crowd of pedestrians.

Depart, take the plunge. After having left the shore behind, for awhile you stay much closer to it than to the one on the other side, at least just enough so that the body starts reckoning and says to itself, silently, that it can always go back. Up to a certain threshold, you hold on to this feeling of security: in other words, you have not really left. On this side of the adventure, your foot, once it has crossed a second threshold, waits expectantly for the approach: you find yourself close enough to the steep bank to say you have arrived. Right bank or left bank, what does it matter, in both cases it is land or ground. You do not swim, you wait to walk, like someone who jumps, takes off, and then lands, but does not remain in flight.

The swimmer, on the contrary, knows that a second river runs in the one that everyone sees, a river between the two thresholds, after or before which all security has vanished: there he abandons all reference points.

Direction
The real passage occurs in the middle. Whatever direction determined by the swim, the ground lies dozens or hundreds of yards below the belly or miles behind and ahead. The voyager is alone. One must cross in order to know solitude, which is signaled by the disappearance of all reference points.

At first, the body relativizes direction: Neither left nor right is important as long as I can hold my ground, it says. But in the middle of the crossing, even the ground is missing; any sense of belonging, of support is gone. Thus the body flies and forgets solidity, not while waiting for stable reunions by any means, but as if it were settling into its foreign life for good: arms and legs enter this weak and fluid carrier, the skin adapts to the turbulent environment, vertigo ceases because the head can count on no support other than its own; under threat of drowning, the body confidently takes up a slow breaststroke.

The outside observer willingly believes that the one who changes passes from one state of belonging to another: standing at Calais as he was at Dover, as if it were merely a question of getting a second passport. No, that would only be true if the middle could be reduced to a point with no dimension, as it is in a jump. The body that crosses surely learns about a second world, the one toward which it is heading, where another language is spoken, but, above all, where the body is initiated into a third world, through which it passes.

The body will never walk or stand erect as it did when it knew only standing still or walking; biped before this event, it is now flesh and fish. It has not only changed banks, language, customs, genre, and species, but it has known the hyphen: frog-man. The first animal belongs, the second animal too, but the strange living thing that will one day enter this white river, which flows in the visible river, and that had to adapt under threat of dying to its eccentric waters has left all sense of belonging behind.

With this new birth, it is now truly exiled. Deprived of a home. A fire with no hearth. Intermediary. Angel. Messenger. Hyphen. Forever outside any community, but a little and just barely in all of them. Harlequin, already.

Birth of the Third

It reaches the other shore: formerly left-handed, you now find that it is right-handed; once Gascon, today francophone or anglophile. You believe it is naturalized, converted, inverted, turned upside down. Of course, you're right. It truly inhabits, albeit painfully, the second shore. Do you think it is single? No, surely, double. Having become right-handed, it remains left-handed. Bilingual does not simply mean that it speaks two languages: it passes unceasingly through the fold of the dictionary. Well-adapted yet loyal to what it was. It has forgotten, as it had to, but it remembers nonetheless. Do you believe it to be double?

If so, you are not taking into account the crossing, the suffering, the courage of apprenticeship, the dread of a probable drowning, the crevice opened in the thorax by the drawing out of the arms, the legs, and the tongue, the wide line of forgetting and memory that marks the longitudinal axis of these infernal rivers that in antiquity were called amnesias. You believe it to be double, ambidextrous, a dictionary, and it is really triple or third, inhabiting both banks and haunting the middle where the two directions converge, as well as the direction of the flowing river, and that of the wind, of the uneasy list of the swim, of the numerous intentions that produce decisions; in this river within the river, or in the crevice in the middle of the body, is formed a compass or a rotunda from which diverge twenty or one hundred thousand directions. Did you believe it to be triple?

You are still mistaken, it is multiple. Source or interchange of directions, relativizing forever the left, the right, and the earth from which these directions emerge, it has incorporated a compass into its liquid body. Do you still think it converted, inverted, turned upside down? Certainly. Even more: universal. On the mobile axis of the river and of the body the source of direction shivers, moved.

Learning

In crossing the river, in delivering itself completely naked to belonging to the opposite shore, it has just learned a third thing. The other side, new customs, a new language, certainly. But above all, it has just discovered learning in this blank middle that has no direction from which to find all directions. At the apex of the cranium, in a vortex, twists the cowlick's tuft, a place/milieu *[lieu/milieu]* where all directions come together.

Universal means what is unique yet versed in all directions. Infinity enters the body of the one who, for a long time, crosses a rather dangerous and large river in order to know those regions where, as on the high seas, whatever direction one adopts or decides, reference points lie equally far. From then on, the solitary soul, wandering without belonging, can receive and integrate everything: all directions are equal. Did he traverse the totality of the concrete to enter abstraction?

Do schoolmasters realize that they only fully taught those they thwarted, or rather, completed, those they forced to cross?

Certainly, I never learned anything unless I left, nor taught someone else without inviting him to leave his nest.

Departure requires a rending that rips a part of the body from the part that still adheres to the shore where it was born, to the neighborhood of its kinfolk, to the house and the village with its customary inhabitants, to the culture of its language and to the rigidity of habit. Whoever does not get moving learns nothing, Yes, depart, divide yourself into parts. Your peers risk condemning you as a separated brother. You were unique and had a point of reference, you will become many, and sometimes incoherent, like the universe, which, it is said, exploded at the beginning in a big bang. Depart, and then everything begins, at least your explosion in worlds apart. Everything begins from this nothing.

No learning can avoid the voyage. Under the supervision of a guide, education pushes one to the outside. Depart: go forth. Leave the womb of your mother, the crib, the shadow cast by your father's house and the landscapes of your childhood. In the wind, in the rain: the outside has no shelters. Your initial ideas only repeat old phrases. Young: old parrot. The voyage of children, that is the naked meaning of the Greek word *pedagogy*. Learning launches wandering.

To break into pieces in order to launch oneself on a road with an uncertain outcome demands such heroism that it is primarily children who are capable of it. But, children must, moreover, be seduced to become engaged in it. To seduce: to lead elsewhere. To split off from the so-called natural direction. No gesture of the hand that holds the racket seeks a pose that the body would spontaneously strike, no English word issues from a form that a French mouth would easily outline, no ideas in geometry follow from wide-open eyes, neither the wind nor the birds teach us music . . . what remains is to seize the body, language, or the soul against the grain. *To split off* necessarily means to begin on a road that cuts across and leads to an unknown place. Above all: never take the easy road, swim the river instead.

Depart. Go out. Allow yourself to be seduced one day. Become many, brave the outside world, split off somewhere else. These are the first three foreign things, the three varieties of alterity, the three initial means of being exposed. For there is no learning without exposure, often dangerous, to the other. I will never again know what I am, where I am, from where I'm from, where I'm going, through where to pass. I am exposed to others, to foreign things.

Through where: that is the fourth question, posed at new cost. The temporary guide and the schoolmaster know the place where they are taking the initiate, who doesn't know it now, and who will discover it in time. This space exists—land, town, language, gesture, or theorem. The voyage is leading there. But the route follows topographical lines, at a rate or along a trajectory that depends both on the legs of the runner and on the terrain he traverses—rockfall, desert or sea, swamp or cliff. He does not hasten, at first, to the end, toward the target, braced in the direction of his goal. No, the game of pedagogy is in no respect a game for two, voyager and destination, but for three. The third place intervenes, there, as the threshold of passage. And, most often, neither the student nor the initiator know where this door is located nor what to do with it.

One day, at some point, everyone passes through the middle of this white river, through the strange state of a phase change, which could be called sensitivity, a word that signifies possibility or capacity in every sense. Sensitive, for example, the scale when it seesaws up and down, vibrating, in the beautiful middle, in both directions; sensitive also the child who will walk when he throws himself into an unbalanced balance; observe him again when he immerses himself in speech, reading, or writing, cleansed, besmirched in sense and nonsense. How hypersensitive we were, stuck-up, sowing our wild oats, when crossing all the thresholds of youth. That state vibrates like an instability, a metastability, like a nonexcluded third between equilibrium and disequilibrium, between being and nothingness. Sensitivity haunts a central and peripheral place—in the form of a star.

Have you ever tended goal for your team, while an adversary hurries to take a clean, close shot? Relaxed, as if free, the body mimes the future participle, fully ready to unwind: toward the highest point, at ground level, or halfway up, in both directions, left and right; toward the center of the solar plexis, a starry plateau launches its virtual branches in all directions at once, like a bouquet of axons. This is the state of vibrating sensitivity—wakeful, alert, watchful—a call to the animal who passes close by, lying in wait, spying, a solicitation in every sense, from every direction for the whole admirable network of neurons. Run to the net, ready to volley: once again a future participle, the racket aims for all shots at once, as if the body, unbalanced from all sides, were knotting a ball of time, a sphere of directions, and were releasing a starfish from its thorax. At the center of the star is hidden the third place, formerly called a soul, experienced by passing through a channel that is difficult to cross. The soul inhabits this pole of sensitivity, of virtual capacity, at the same time that it throws itself forward and holds back, that is, that it launches itself halfway, the length of the floating branches of the astral body that explores space, like a sun.

Brain

If the body or the soul knows this, the brain cannot be unaware of it. Asleep or awake, the brain vibrates and jumps in all directions at once so that the complex curve that it leaves on the map of the electroencephalogram expresses or imitates its autonomy in the form of a ball or a bouquet or billions of stars: under the cranial vault constellations twinkle. Sensitive in multiple ways, the body goes up to the net to volley or, an expert goalie, gets ready to receive shots from every angle of the space and at any moment . . . An overall balance, a child audacious enough to leap into an uncertain undertaking, a mouth that will stammer between noise and speech, between Yes and No, clarity and darkness, lies and truth, tongue, lips, and palate sheltering this included third. The brain is busy mapping this space-time: How? Seemingly from being here and elsewhere at once, continuously and discontinuously. Skipping or twinkling, it haunts this third place discovered in swimming across the river.

As with intelligence, so with the promise of invention . . . Remain this player for a long time, this child, this watcher, who balances or swims, this virgin getting ready to decide. Body, muscles, nerves, direction and sensitivity, soul, brain and knowledge, all converge in this third place in the shape of a star: watch out on the left, pass on the right, keep watch from above, and run below . . . .

It—the third place—is sown in time and space. In the middle of the window through which it passes, the body knows that it has crossed to the outside, that it has just entered another world. Space and our stories are full of such thresholds: the axis of the river, the arm of the sea, through which one swims. Here the adventure seems to come to an end, whereas the voyage has merely reached one stage of it; the third included certainly, because here something simultaneously ends and does not end. This is the site of the wall, which varies according to the day and the climber, where the third discovers that, this morning, he will get through, even if the storm breaks. The third included: not arrived, yet parvenu. This is the point in labor when, suddenly, as if by magic, everything becomes easy and one doesn't know why. Right in the middle, the work is over. This is the moment where years of training, of will, of tenacity suddenly enter and settle into the corporeal schema or categorial ease; this very noon I simultaneously begin and have finished, I know that I will speak Chinese though I don't speak it yet, that I will solve the equations of the problem, recover my health, finish the crossing. So real, this threshold, that it can fool you: here is the summit where the route begins, though the beginner believes that at last there are no more obstacles; false middle, imaginary third, sometimes.

Birth and Knowledge

Something compels me to say that we were already subjected to the four major pedagogical tests or exposures—the break up of the body into parts, the expulsion to the outside, the need to choose a sideways and paradoxical path, finally the passage through the third place—in the first hours of our birth, when it was necessary, not without shedding blood sometimes, or crushing our heads, to wrench ourselves from the body with which our being was integrated, since we had lived only as part of the maternal body. It was necessary to suffer an irresistible push toward the unbreathable cold of the outside, to follow a path that no previous constraint had predicted, finally to pass through a narrow, recently dilated passage, all ready to close up again, at the risk of suffocating, of being strangled, of dying of asphyxia in the obstructed, stenotic, restrained, closed passageway . . . So that, everyone, like me, simply because he is alive knows that, all of that: those death throes in order to be born, that death to live again elsewhere, that is to say here, in another time, that is to say now, and that, because he is there, standing with beating heart, panting, he already knows, therefore can adapt, learn—die-live with the third included.

We all came out through that pass, that foreign and natural mountainous place where the highest point of the low points is exactly equal to the lowest point of the high points. We learned, already, that the experience of death throes could suddenly equal the very article of living. Birth, knowledge: what more terrible exposure to the most formidable danger?

In the course of these experiences, time springs neither from assuming a position (the equilibrium of the statue) nor from opposition, a second stability from which nothing can come, nor from their relation—an arch or static arc of perpetual immobility—but from a deviation from equilibrium that throws or launches position outside of itself, toward disequilibrium, which keeps it from resting, that is, from achieving a precarious balance: everyday language expresses it exactly with the word *exposure*. In the axis of the river whose current flares, the swimmer is exposed, just like anyone who takes any kind of risk.

Time is exposed, and in space springs forth from places where there is no being-there. Space is sown with sites of exposure where time is deployed.

Slippery, the third place exposes the passerby. But no one passes, no one gets through without this slippage. No one, nothing in the world, has ever changed without just managing not to fall. All evolution and learning require passing through the third place. So that knowledge, thought, or invention does not cease to pass from one third place to another and therefore is always exposed, or so that the one who knows, thinks, or invents quickly becomes a passing third. Neither *positioned* nor *opposed,* unceasingly *exposed.* Rarely balanced, rarely also unbalanced, always deviating from the place, wandering with no fixed habitat. The passing third is characterized by the nonplace, yes, by broadening, that is, liberty, better yet, by a precarious balance—the constraining and sovereign condition of bearing toward the true.

So the third-instructed whose instruction never stops has almost been described: through his experiences and by nature, he has just entered time; he has abandoned his place, his being and his there, the village of his birth; expelled from paradise, he has crossed numerous rivers, with all their risks and dangers. Now he is taking off from the earth itself: does he inhabit time?

No, no one inhabits time, because it excludes the thirds and evicts everyone, immediately. That is why, from now on, we all live evicted.

Writing

During this pedagogic voyage, I would therefore not advise anyone to leave a left-handed child free to use his hand, especially to write.

Extraordinary work, writing mobilizes and recruits such a refined group of muscles and neurological endings that all delicate manual activity, whether in optics or watchmaking, is cruder by comparison. To teach this specialized skill to a population makes of it, first of all, a collective of adroit people—note in passing the word with which the right-handed ruling class mounts an advertising campaign for hemiplegics.[1] They could become brain surgeons, precision mechanics, do anything: discovering highly precise muscular and nervous dexterity leads to subtle thinking.

To enter the world anew by inverting your body requires a shattering abandonment. My life is reduced, perhaps, to the memory of that rending moment when the body explodes in parts and traverses a transverse river where the waters of memory and forgetting flow. One part is torn away and another remains. A discovery and opening up whose deferred healing a whole professional life of writing later describes.

Does this scar faithfully follow the old suture of body and soul? Does the thwarted left-hander become ambidextrous? No, rather a crossbred body, like a chimera. Left-handed when it comes to scissors, the hammer, the scythe, the foil, the ball, the racket, the expressive gesture if not society—this, the body—the left-hander has never stopped belonging to the maladroit, sinister minority, as Latin has it; hurray for the Greek language, which dubs this minority aristocratic! But right-handed for the pen and the fork, he shakes the right hand upon being introduced—this, the soul. He is properly brought up for public life, but left-handed for caresses and private life. Those complete organisms have their hands full.

How, finally, can tolerance and nonviolence be acquired, except by placing oneself in the other's shoes, knowing from the other side?

I would not advise anyone to deprive a child of this adventure, of crossing the river, of this wealth, of this treasure that I was never able to use up, because it contains the potential of learning, the universe of tolerance and the solar twinkling of attention. The so-called thwarted left-handers live in a world only half explored by most. They know limits and lack, and I am fulfilled: a lateral hermaphrodite.

---

1. *Adroit* contains the word *droit*, which in French means right.—Trans.

Sex

Only some living things have the pleasure of a sex, whereas everything, in the world, whether animate or inanimate, is provided with a direction. Direction goes further, deeper than sex. Left and right apply to more things than male or female and make more universal distinctions than does gender.

The stars turn and advance, oriented, like particles around the nucleus of an atom. Crystals and molecules are lateralized, with highly refined symmetries and asymmetries. Direction or orientation comes neither from men nor from their preferences, from their inclinations, but from the inanimate world that precedes the living and from the living that precedes culture. Things lean to one side: force fields, boreal auroras, twisting turbulences, cyclones, spots on the planet Jupiter . . . the universal was born, it is said, from spontaneous symmetry breaking.[2] Direction traverses the immensity of the sky, enters the box of details, and rides on the arrow of time. Then it passes to the shellfish, levogyres, dextrogyres, to the crustaceans that display a large claw next to the smaller one, heterocercal in that regard, then to all bodies—to ours, our eyes, the flanges of our nostrils, the cowlick, and to the somewhat disrupted balance of the female bosom: at least statistically speaking, the left breast is bigger than the right. Direction traverses our bodies and settles in fabricated objects. The left-hander finds his way with difficulty in the forest of right-handed technology.

Orientation, finally, conforms to our preferences, to our cultural divisions, to the reds in power and the whites on the bench, or vice versa, through the revolving assembly. Politics, the latest and least significant offshoot, repeats the pattern frantically. Were I to be condemned in the court of sociology for not having said that the world is oriented only through the projection of its divisions or the imposition of its choices, I believe I would answer, Yet, it does turn. Everywhere, the world is lateralized; that's the way it is.

Orientation goes from the local to the global and from the small to the large, from atoms to stars, from inanimate matter to living

---

2. The effect of an unpredictable reduction in symmetry in a physical system as that system changes to one of lower energy.—TRANS.

matter, from crystals to shellfish, from nature to culture, from the pure to the applied, from space to time, from things to languages; thus it traverses, as well, and without difficulty, the passage(ways) that philosophy reputes to be the most delicate.

Now, division by gender concerns only sexed living things, some social roles, sometimes language. In the end, very little.

Everyone, unconscious of what they are saying, says that the compass, indicating the North, allows you to orient yourself. What if I, an Aquitanian, a Californian, a Southwesterner, decided to occident myself from the South? Or: go right straight ahead, they say, without taking into account that rightly one should tack to the starboard. How can justice present itself according to the promotional image of the balanced scale, when the word *right* itself makes it lean to one side? Here compelled by the incline, what is said is not inclined by gender.

In summary, sex weighs less than direction, the male less than the right. We are more consistently plunged into the lateralized vortex than into sexual emotion. This comparison designates the experience of a thwarted or completed left-hander (who is at the center of the first division) as being more intense and of greater breadth than the mythic one of the androgyne at the center of the second. The former goes as far as the object, from crystals to stars, while the Hermaphrodite stops at the flesh. The second division, revolving around itself, is necessarily narcissistic; the first opens onto the world and therefore is knowledgeable.

Nothing in nature, then, either inanimate or living, or in culture, either verbal or visual, refers to a space or a time that is homogeneous or isotropic, reversible, that one can divide in an equal or symmetrical manner, perfectly, at one's leisure. There is no such thing as balanced indifference. There is no center or axis; it cannot be found, or it is absent.

Orientation can thus be said to be originary, invariable, irreducible, so constantly physical that it becomes metaphysical. Through it, universal, we communicate with the universe that was born, I repeat, of this ancient *clinamen,* which has been rejuvenated, in our contemporary sciences, under the name of spontaneous symmetry breaking.

Leibniz even assimilates orientation to the raison d'être of things: they exist rather than nothing. One can thus describe the principle of reason as a differential of direction and outline it using a very small arrow departing from the absent and unlocatable center to direct itself someplace. Therefore, its angle appears, like a flash of lightning, in improbable places and times.

Whence the ambidextrous person has no raison d'être: nil, beneath direction, at zero, undecided, flat, uncoded, ill because he has no lack. The right-hander or left-hander lives in a half world and goes to sleep in one direction, on one side, leaning into one half. Fractional but justified by their raison d'être; in addition, blind to their dead complement, deprived of a potential link to the other sense; the male seeks the female who calls, and sex shines with desire for the unifying moment, whereas the division of direction is devoid of this desire. Nothing allows us to hope on the right for an encounter with the left; the dotted line toward it is effaced. The hermaphrodite, rare, is encountered as frequently as sex, even bad sex, or females who are pregnant . . . whereas the complete body sleeps on both ears, it cannot turn itself over, nor can it ever be converted. A full universe, one with itself, or the sum of halves.

The ambidextrous person, neutral; the two others, halves; only the thwarted left-hander makes for fulfillment and unity. Zero; two halves; an undivided individual. A world or rather a universe, fragments, or nothing. Whoever is not a completed left-hander is condemned to analysis because he lives in division and destruction.

Whoever finds himself complete neither sees nor senses a limit and therefore does not understand cutting, lack, the frantic desire to transgress an inaccessible frontier of whose location he is uncertain. It took me a long time to understand my indescribable luck in being unable to understand these eccentricities.

Like the one, for example, that consists of repeating that every society is founded on exchange. No: the straight, asymmetrical, more elementary arrow incontestably gives the parasite the first, dangerous, tragic, exposed place. Legal right is required, at least, and morality, on top of that, to patiently construct the double arrow of globally balanced exchanges. Everywhere and always orientation begins; what remains to be constructed are the different balancing acts. Exchange, then, comes second.

From writing with a pen, our era is moving on to keyboards. How many composers lack the left hand! They say it accompanies: a servant, a slave, a shadow of the other. No, hands in the network of notes make love to each other; what a barbarous custom to leave one almost passive! Sometimes these composers are androgynous in miraculous scores that allow them to be heard truly bilaterally.

The piano itself figures a complete body, completely flat, everywhere coded, the body resembles this very soundboard. Cut keyboards, broken soundboards where one can read only fragments or analyses, bass pianos whose high notes would be lost in the gray, effaced by the clouds, treble instruments whose bass would be forgotten in the deepest shadows—these are the left-handed or the right-handed. And, tomorrow, we will write not only with this one hand that holds the pencil and pen over a page, oriented or disoriented, but with two complementary hands on keyboards or other consoles. The question of writing is thereby changed: with luck, we will also be able to form right-handers completed by their left hand. We leave the rightist civilization of style to enter that of keyboards—planarian, voluminous, and decentered civilization. That will change us, body and soul, and that will transform time.

Chimera

Where does the center of the piano ring? Around the third A? Hear the *x* or the *chi* of the scale mounting from left to right, encountering toward some midpoint the cascade of notes running from high to low, listen to the chimera and the point of overlap. At this scaled, vernal point lies the crossroads, under the statue of Hermaphrodite; this springlike place is located in the body, I know it as pain and fountain, scar and source, treasure and secret fold, a bond passes through there as a bandage for a second path and that path as the ligature of the first. Do not tear off the chimera's dressing.

Our ancestors searched, precisely, for this mysterious place where the body is knotted to the soul, for the bonds and folds of this knot.

The thwarted left-hander resembles a chimera that would carry his soul on the right, because he writes from the side of cultural works, and his body on the left because there he holds his tools for the work that earns him a living; here is a continuous world, passing through his entrails, which unites the living and pure culture, a hand to work the fields or harvest the grain, a hand to write with a refined style or to compose music, an interchange through the vernal site where bodily labor normally persists, by way of the bandage, in highly abstract thought.

This complete, I mean to say normal, monster—unicorn, sphinx, woman-serpent, or siren—constructs a connected universe, passing through the overlaps of the center, which unites private life and the collective exterior, a hand for caresses, a side for the sign and the greeting, where the space of play and refined seriousness touch and are mixed, left for the ball and right for the pen, a passage to the scaled point where the sense of sensation is transmuted into the sense of signification, where solitude opens up, where freed attention becomes productive, where laughter will be mixed with tears, where rigor is refined into beauty.

The thwarted-completed left-hander slides constantly across the bandage or the connection, practices one hundred times a day the interchange through which industrious sweat goes toward the singularities of art, through which stupid and stubborn effort blossoms into a work, through which the rotting fermentations of the earth end up in the universal of pure form. Liger or tiglon, the issue of a tigress and a lion, or of a tiger and a lionness, respectively, half-breed, Harlequin, crossbred animal, trained from the beginning in the academic right, still gauche in everyday, basic life, binds, knots, sews, articulates, heals, harmonizes, has had to die a thousand deaths to get there, torn up beneath his derisory dressing, his soul a lake of tears in the center of his thorax, he built his game with two hands, crossing, crossing again, caressing and signing this vernal, healed middle—new solid, serene, younger than aged childhood.

You need a cross to locate a center and a difficult path to get there. A single line right straight ahead or a single side are not enough. You need a crossbred body, passing via the organs in the center, heart, stomach, solar plexus, sexual organ, tongue, a nose with wisdom and taste, traversing the reconnaissance of axial places, in order for language to really begin, for sex to appear: how can the left-handed, the right-handed, divided, mark their center, supine as they are, in one set position? The set, or direction, of the wind does not make a compass card. Many sets are necessary, and they must cross each other in the center of the compass, so that meaning/direction will spring forth. Do the right- and left-handed have a sex, a language, how do they, the unfortunates, occupy the multiply crossed compass of their brain?

A heavily underlined border of the body—so strongly extant that it takes itself for a reference, pulls everything to itself, loses the center—could be called the border of gravity, always brought, like a decentered ball, to rest on the ground on the same side: a tumbler. Even the global mass, strong and dark there, fades little by little in the grayness as one moves away from that side, until it floats, almost absent, a light weight, with a high-pitched tone. What is lateralized resembles a flag shivering in the wind. Its body has rare lands, unknown places, places where the map is white. How else to say, whatever clarity or value one grants the nuances, that its center, chiaroscuro, partakes of the conscious and the unconscious? Divided tongue, cut sexual organ. Either the sexual organ is cut, a section, or it is crossed, an intersection. A cut body and a crossbred body do not define an equivalent center, or even the same animal.

The two strips or paths meet in the third place of intersection, single, double, and crossed: absent, excluded, powerfully present. The brain is single, double, and crossed, like a chiasmus, like a chimera: through the brain, a model of the body, we think, at least on the organic level. The thwarted left-hander has a body modeled on his own brain, a complete organism that returns unceasingly to the central model, in the form of a cross. And to all of its axial organs.

Similarly single and double and crossed, sex is thus named "section," because its division must bring to the fore the light and the dark, the conscious on the strong side and the unconscious on the weak side, as is usually the case in lateralized people; or sex can be understood as an intersection, as a double orientation. The great cross of the chimera draws and produces this intersection that, also, means product. Luminous discovery: direction produces sex, the two directions are its factors. Desire, in the middle, is the sharp, incisive, live encounter of these two directions that form the world and make us participate in it.

The brain is single, double, and crossed, intersection and product. Sex is single, double, and crossed. Language, in the center, is single, double, and crossed, and, made to be translated, to sing the chimeric, it always whispers doubt and trebles. Forked, the tongue bifurcates, speaks in two voices, in two senses. It, too, is produced by direction. Bass, treble, strong or weak, light, dark, true or false, rigorous, imaginary, lying or loyal, foreign or vernacular, attractive, repugnant, always polarized. Sensible, nonsensical *[Sensé, insensée]*. But, suddenly, passing from one direction *[sens]* to another and, from there, to non-sense, through a third place.

Fold and Knot

I do not know, I know what takes place in the center. I know the overlap, I named it the bandage, the cross or the crossing. Which strip passes over, which under?

This elementary question is posed when one takes two threads in hand and gets ready to tie a knot, an ancient practice, in seafaring or weaving, or, in the theory of graphs, rather new. Below, above. One would say that we are playing hot potato. Penelope the weaver intertwined the stitches in this way: over, under. Every complex knot is resolved in so many local folds where the same question is again posed: above, below? Another way of linking the left and the right, you only have to lean a little to notice it right away. The two hands, complementary, weave or knit together just as a moment ago they were competing/converging on the keyboards. Single and double, they cross: in what sense? Before teaching children the console or the keyboard give them something to weave or knit.

Now then, if one follows language attentively, the term *complex*, coming from fold or knot, designates and even describes a situation that is a bit more constrained than multiplication. Dedicated only to the number, the latter cares nothing for place, whereas the term complex takes it into account. Complex designates a group of folds when it passes from arithmetic, pure counting, to topology, which has a penchant for crumpled bits of cloth.

After all, the complex never described anything but this kind of situation, and, in physics, for example, a network, electrical or otherwise, where numerous threads pass one over the other and some under certain others—these to the left or the right of those as much as you like—the outline of a combinatorial topology, a systemic knot, named complex for the first time by J. B. Listing, in

German, and used by Maxwell in his theory of electrical fields. Such a network of threads or of forces—sometimes intercepted by resistors or capacitors—is usually called a Wheatstone bridge by physicists.

When such a bridge is balanced between two limits, no measuring device can detect it. Thus the complex cannot be observed: neither seen nor known. Extant then, enormous and sometimes troubling, difficult to comprehend, intertwined, but yet knotted in and by this nullity of difference in potential, it only exists as capacity, as a black memory, a middle between presence and absence, forgetting and memory, local energy and global incapacity. Discovered there, the unconscious, admirable network of strange stitches and knots, it is part of the logical family of thirds. If it exists, it lies toward the middle and, like it, has a tendency to get lost in the blackness of memory, then to occupy all of space and time.

First Memories

Day. During the day, Penelope weaves, composes, builds her tapestry, in keeping with the lost cartoon no one talks about, but which follows the plan and makes the scenes of the voyage appear: the island of Circe, Nausicaa, who throws her ball on the beach, blind Polyphemous in the hollows of the cave, the bare-breasted Sirens surrounding the straits of enchantment . . . piece by piece, day after day, a loom for his lover, a stage in the journey for her lover, a fragment of song for the bard or the troubadour, dozens of verses for Homer, as if all four produced together, in daylight, one his course under sail, the other her scene on woven cloth, the writer his page in columns, the singer his score for the melody—to each his daily task.

We follow, listen, read, look at the various paintings, immersed in the incantation of the music: the fatal magician, the young girl with her attendants, the one-eyed monster, and, arranged beneath the wind of the melody, lips opened by the silent wind of voices, the female fish with high breasts on the water, lit by the sun.

Night. Now, when the sun falls beneath the horizon, when the sailor furls the sails and the lyre is quiet, when the night impedes the genius from writing and the reader from reading and seeing, they say that Penelope undoes the woven piece, that she effaces Circe, then her island, that the ball in front of Nausicaa's arm disappears, that Cyclops loses his only eye: the threads unravel, the cloth disappears, the notes fall from a fraying staff. The shadow brings these phantoms, the melody infiltrates silence . . . one no longer sees the Sirens nor the aphonic and musical mouth nor the charming breasts displayed above the flowing swell.

This ending signifies that we have need of neither canvas nor map nor printed score nor written poem, nor doubtless of memory. Life and our black entrails are enough. The piece woven yesterday, each suite of measures and strophes entered clearly into our flesh and dark forgetfulness, buried alive in the shadow of the body or the dark soul, for the night of epochs and without taking up room, no more of a burden than an arm or another organ. One can undo them without causing damage. They remain there without being there. The night remembers the day without containing it; this nothing remembers something; memory, which is musical, does not take up room. The voices enter in silence, and there they work, in the dark, in the light of intelligence.

Our suppleness contains the unraveled tapestry, the absent cartoons and the tacit melody, with no other burden than that of the muscles, nerves of the heart. Dissolved, memory is made flesh, it comes part way back to life, already vibrant, rising from the black sea.

Morning. I believe I never heard them sung, no old grandmother told them to me, I only saw a fleeting profile once, I only read a bad summary, yet my body, this morning, with no difficulty, restores, brought up from the sea and those deep grottoes, the enormous ewes that come out of the black lair of the one-eyed monster, the disturbing Circe who makes sailors emerge from foul pigs, the ball that bounds, dancing, outside the melee into which Nausicaa's attendants throw themselves, the mute Sirens with high breasts on the singing waves.

All are resuscitated from the empty tomb, from unknotted threads, from effaced verses, from silence, from my loins, from absence, from calm and living flesh, from my sonorous thorax emerging from the dark sea.

You who hear or witness these figures looming in the shadows in the exquisite light of music, in the rhythmic narrative or the scansion of the weaving, boldly forget them this evening, undo in yourself without regret the threads that hold them or the notes and the words that evoke them. One day you will hum them by heart for your grandchildren, understanding that evening, at last, what you had once learned blindly: the magic fairy and the naive girl playing ball, a dangerous one-eyed thing or a blind victim, and the choral Sirens, tacit, with pale breasts above the water.

Forgotten in our bodies, the Sirens remember; they sing the poem. Without space, music holds in us the nil island of memory. The third place around which the rhythm beats and the music vibrates disappears in the flesh, without leaving a trace.

Rose Window

What takes place in the center trembles and vibrates in time.

The volleyer and the goalie know how to wait for and to favor at one and the same moment the low shot, the thundering burst toward a distant point, the rapid and short throw, the high jump, the brusque act of avoidance if the attack comes from the front . . . left, right, above, below, how do their limbs come unknotted? How, I do not know, but I know that the body knows how to do it, because it sleeps and watches on both ears.

It settles, unbalanced, at a distance, from all sides. Thus, it knows how to maintain concentration. Free of direction. With unknotted, floating threads, all knots open and uncut, arms and legs white, head empty; circular like a rotunda, high like a plateau that is not inclinded, the body becomes, if I dare say it, possible. Immobile, with the capacity to move. The tapestry we just referred to is being unknotted. One would say the bright spot, radiating in all directions, of the rose window of a cathedral.

Attentive, in waiting, the body positions itself *[se pose]*. The philosophers call a thesis the act of positing *[poser]* an object, a fact, a true affirmation. The body does not assume this kind of pose *[ne se pose pas]*, like a stone or a statue that is immobilized according to the laws of static, resting on its pedestal and around its center of gravity, stable, balanced, abandoned to the rules of rest. Movement has been described as a series of equilibria, as a sequence of reposes.

The body is like a statue when it sleeps and becomes one after death. In both cases, it reposes, sometimes lying on one side. Left-handed on the left side, right-handed on the other. Standing up, my legs feel heavy and my head rather light. The skin of my feet sometimes blemished with corns, fleeting ideas, words emitted by my breath. As if maintaining equilibrium of itself produced divisions that have long been disputed in the philosophical arena. The spiritual, light, partakes of the soft breath; the real, portentous, of the weighty. Do the opinionated do nothing more than argue over a vague sentiment that issues from the body itself?

Now if the body plays the part of a statue, with its weight, toward the bottom, it sculpts a second one, through its lateralization, to the right or the left. It rests on its feet, but drawn to one side. It would be necessary to trace a composing oblique line that would give the true vertical line of the living being who is unceasingly attracted by this diagonal, and which would form the angle of its own fall with the normal line. Everything leans and is exposed on the side where it will fall.

If you're considered realistic you're said to have your feet on the ground. Your feet, not your hands, or your head. What is important lies below. They forget to ask you which foot first: left or right? Which one, unique and definitively decided on, do you already have in the grave? This is literally the statue of the body proper, leaning like some antique colossus, one leg launched forward to give the illusion of walking. This is its usual thesis: repose. It sleeps stretched out on one side, one foot first. Here the forces of death are drawn.

On the contrary, it gets up, wakes up; attentive, it waits. Emerging from rest, it no longer allows itself to be overcome: it is open to any eventuality. What is coming can come from each direction on the horizon. It is careful then to efface all the forces that were making it into a posed statue, a static thesis. Yet it does not move, but effaces the fatal angle of the fall, minimizes its gravity as best it can by inundating its muscular elasticity with subjectivity, quickly forgets that it is leaning in one direction and assumes a different pose—a tennis player readying for the volley, an alert goalie, a watcher. It fills its space equally: high as much as low, right as much as left, it abandons preferences and determinations, its memberships, and knows the better how to do so because it has often crossed the old white river. Here it is, a completed body.

From which one can see that the opinionated one, who cries for the left or the right, or for the real ground or for the spiritual height, is truly not paying attention. He does not defend himself, as a son once asked of his father the king, on the left and on the right.[3] The watcher who spies or the assiduous seeker, suspended, immediately becomes a thwarted left-hander.

Who, on the contrary, always pays attention, fulfilled by the virtual, overflowing with possiblity and with capacity; he is literally nothing but potential: he is exposed in all directions, like a small sun. During his passion he has effaced all the forces that determine him, or, rather, completed them. Neither angel nor beast, since the double negation produces a stupid and worthless neutral thing, but angel and beast at once, wandering without belonging, a mixed body, reaching the possible. What exists is first possible. The body enters into capacity. More precisely, it increases in capacity, moves upstream of every turn to action. Here let us not call it the undecided body, though it is placed upstream of every decision, though it precedes the cut. Indecision speaks of a malady downstream and predecision of the capacity of the source. Pre-cise (before the incision)—that can be said in better words: virgin. The attentive body blanched like virgin snow. Attentiveness and waiting go upstream toward whiteness. The whole body seeks the neighborhood of the center in order to coil up in the possible. Impossible? It inhabits these small reduced models: brain, sex, language, small crossbred bodies. It goes after the fold of the crossing, the site where directions are exchanged together, like lap dissolves. If you change direction, you are obliged to pay attention. This resembles the sun of rose windows: exposure in all directions.

Harlequin becomes Pierrot.

The brain, the sexual organ, the tongue expose possibilities in waiting, themselves organs or functions of the possible. At the crossing

---

3. A reference to the Battle of Poitiers in 1356 during which Philip the Brave fought alongside his father, John the Good, and told him whether to guard his left or right flank—TRANS.

point, the question of the knot, left, right, below, above, is no longer posed, rather, its form is exposed. The crossroads, open, unlocked, translucent to its own routes, belongs to all the paths, in a stable and unstable manner. White place, star-shaped traffic circle, floating. Everything quivers around the axis or the transparent center and in its neighboring regions. The brain waits, an immense complex of surveillance, multiply oscillating, trembling, vibrating in time like its own electroencephalogram. The sexual organ hesitates, white with waiting and capacity; shining indeed with stength, it beats; the tongue doubts and gets entangled, reticent, white with possibility, like a plateau that is not inclined, oscillating like music and the sounds that carry it, sparkling.[4]

A series of trembles, essential marks and, maybe, the secret, of life whose birth can be recognized in vibrations—the regular flutterings of the heart or the chaotically erratic and complex twitching of the mind and of the nervous system.

Trill, Music
Let us return to the small, differential arrow, the miniscule, fundamental, divergence of our raison d'être. To lie down on the left or the right side, passive, distances us a good deal from this arrow. Disquiet, minute, shivers near the absent center: the originary divergence from rest. Right-handers like left-handers sleep set deeply in bed [*lit*] with one side dead, as is the case in the set of the wind [*lit du vent*] or the dead branch of a stream. The left-hander must be exposed to the right and the right-hander to the left to be woken from their animal quietude or their mortal slumber, to warm their rigidity. This done, they pass through the center.

Whosoever departs from one shore and leaves it behind but holds on to it in order to try to reach and inhabit—adopt—the opposite shore, passes through the axis so that the body experiences the tearing in the thorax or the belly, in the middle of the mouth or between the eyes, made by the originary arrow. Torn to pieces by the arrow's span, exposed. Since the body haunts the left

4. In French the word *sexe* can mean both sexual organ and sex, as the word *langue* means both language and tongue.—TRANS.

and right banks at once, it must cross unceasingly; thus its life, its time, and its natural place vibrate, tremble, shiver, shudder, vacillate, hesitate, doubt around the anxious fault line, always awake, ringing like a vibrating cord.

The originary orientation comes from the absent and unlocatable center as if it were taking root there: the flash that signals it and hides it with its bursts and eclipses twinkles everywhere like a small sun.

We do not find the center, and we are inclined to abandon it. We lean to the right, to the left, to get away from it. Are we afraid of it? We neither know how to nor can we inhabit this fault line, this axis or this vortex: who would build his house in the middle of a current? No institution, no system, no science, no language, no gesture or thought is founded on this mobile place—which is the ultimate foundation and founds nothing.

We can only head toward it, but, at the very moment of reaching it, we abandon it, compelled by the arrows that depart from it. We spend only an infinitesimal moment there. Time and site of extreme attentiveness.

We turn around. With the same effort and with the same élan, with the same movement, we head toward it, but in the opposite direction. And, once again, carried away, we pass the moment of reaching it. We only spend a short time there. Therefore we turn around. We take up the same path, the opposite way, attracted by this absence, and indefinitely repelled by it. We turn around again. We traverse the river without respite, obliquely or diagonally or transversely, in all possible directions of space and time, return, go, from right to left, from front to back, from low to high, above, below.

Thus are born rhythm, scales, measures, lullabies, familiar refrains, nursery rhymes, music, ritornellos, threnodies, in double time and with two feet, with four feet or in triple time, short, long, short again, feminine rhymes, masculine rhymes, entangled or alternated, the dance, the waltz, the even and the odd, the games of *ilinx*, or vertigo, the hammock on the sea in turbulent pitching and rolling, prayers and rites, the bell that regularly sounds, all vibrations prior to language, all movements crossing and recrossing the absent center where none can ever rest, between nothingness and being, the pole or ultimate foundation that supports nothing except at a distance from itself, this is why experience, existence and ecstasy are expressed by the same word *exposure,* which says distance to equivalence . . . drunkenness, ravishment crowning the geminate shock of love. Sun.

Everything follows from the third place in both directions / senses.

Dance: Minuet of the Third Place

Men and women dance together face to face, but each respective line slowly comes undone, so that each woman is placed in front of the empty space between two men and sees only it, while each man responds only to the same lack between two women. Every woman pretends to love this hole in space, whereas the men recount their love for the absence of women surrounded by women. This way each is alone in his lukewarm sufficiency and his unhappiness.

Then, tired of suffering, each opens his arms, as supplicants used to do, and each hand encounters a hand to his left and another to his right: a sort of alternating, crossed chain is formed. Each person maintains an amorous rapport with the two corresponding dancers who border the space that each understands as part of his destiny, but since the two others, as well, have a relation to the two shadows that frame their space, in front of them, no one sees anyone or speaks to anyone and no one answers them: this chain of supplications produces the multiplication of the need to supplicate. Double slash. From which follow the figures of the dance, through stations and crossings, and their infinite substitutions.

An elementary stitch or thread of real human relations—never straight but made of multiple arabesques, twists, curls, or helixes in the bedroom or the living room, or in the squares—this quincuncial chain resembles a staff where the notes would occupy pretty much the same place, enabling one to hear a familiar form in a regular rhythm, gallop, tango, bebop, minuet; the monotonous murmuring emanates from the line—continuous since our world has been a world—and sings of the indefinite sickness of love.

Central figure of the dance. The third philosophy likes mixed bodies. *Post coitum omne animal triste;* that, in effect, defines the animal very well: what becomes sad after coitus.

Thus man is whatever laughs after coitus.

Magnificence
I recognize in myself a tranquil and stable being-there, a dense nucleus that does not move, as if it resembled my center of gravity or were assembled there. Subject certainly, because nothing lies under it; it is positioned, set down at the lowest point. The body itself lies down or coils around this lowered position, but when it gets up, leaps, jumps, walks, runs or swims, throws the ball or evolves, holds a tool or looks, travels or pays attention, knows, invents, it still turns in relation to this point.

Who am I first of all? This black stone. This stone, a surbased weight that results from vectors of laziness and homebody passivities, heads toward the center of the Earth. Though located in various places, men as a whole only enjoy one being-there, which determines their genus or their species, a unique root of life and of signs that ascribes to man the name *humus*. This weighty arrow is directed toward death, a communal one, lodged no doubt in the same center.

Be on the alert! Watch out! A given event, this mood, a project or thought passes, requires, solicits: in this way a gap arises. Precisely the divergence of walking: the child goes to seek its fortune in the world, launches one foot in relation to the other foot that is set down, rooted, a root directed toward the center of the Earth even though it covers a locality.

Through a disequilibrium free of cares, with no guarantees, with an inchoate disquiet, laughing and risky, being has just dumped the *there*. It is exposed. It abandons abasement and rises up. Grows and launches its branch. Jumps. It leaves what is stable and moves away. Walks, runs. It leaves the shore and takes off. Swims. It abandons habit to experiment. It evolves. Gives. Offers. Loves. Passes the ball. Forgets its own home, climbs, travels, wanders, gets to know, looks, invents, thinks. No longer repeats. I think or I love, therefore I am not; I think or love, therefore I am not me; I think or I love, therefore I am no longer there. I have cast off from being there.

Let's measure the span between the left foot and the right foot, the height of the jump, the unevenness of the path, the breadth of the views, the volume of knowledge, the space that wandering outlines, the map of the traversed desert. This distance separates the animal from the tree and the tree from the stable sand. Being-there takes root in this place near the common center of the world and weighs in at the lowest point of this axis; one would say it was a vegetable. To open distance to this immobile equilibrium projects a second point or place that one must surely call exposed: a gap that invents a space between position and exposure. Distance or gap no longer refer to the center of the Earth nor to the community of invariance and weight.

Who am I? First this stable position that cannot be uprooted. Tree or vegetable, some kind of green. What am I next? I am no longer there, I am not me, I expose myself: I am that exposure. I am toward the other step, no longer in rootedness, but at the extremities, made mobile by the wind, at the branchings, on the summit of the mountain, at the other end of the world from which I depart, in an animal movement, crawling, flight, running . . . I am also that which I know, question, or think, whether a statue, a circle, or you whom I love.

Finally who am I, as a whole? The totality of the volume between being-there and the exposed point, between the position set down in this place, a thesis that is most often low, and exposure. This distance covers at least the whole tree and, sometimes, an immense space. I call this large dimension the soul.

Magni-ficat anima mea: this magnitude, literally, produces, constructs my soul. Always in proportion to exposure. Great souls are very exposed, pusillanimous ones very little. Joy fills them, completes them, just as misery and pain can give them greater depth.

Let us call magnificence the labor in the thorax of this divergence—whether of mediocre or ample size or volume—between the two poles of the position: the low and stable point of the place or the there positioned, set down, on the one hand, and the high point, the nonplace or the enlargement of the soul, risk or liberation, explosion. There is no animal or animated being without these two points, no human being, even a petty one, who has not traveled in this gap. Death is a return to being-there, down below.

Describing, exactly measured, the construction of the soul, at the very moment when it is formed, through dilation or labor in the uterus of a new space beneath the force of a living being equivalent to the word, the psalm names these two points: the humility of the servant, for the low part, thereby evoking the humus, thus man at the same time as the earth; and for the Very High, the sanc-

tity of God. It is not unreasonable, in effect, to call God the infinite
totality of all the points of exposure. In return, he produces great
things in me: *fecit mihi magna* . . . words that repeat the *magni-ficat*
identically, but reverse their order. God magnifies my soul; my soul
magnifies God; the separation between nothing and everything—
magnitude makes God and my soul.

Joy, Dilation, Begetting

Standing on this ladder, the servant measures two times the volume
in formation: from below, with his joy, exultation, exaltation—the
vertical names of exposure; from above, with the glance that God
himself casts, behind him, on his humility. Height is thus measured
twice, directly and inversely. An almost metrical result: the space of
the soul occupies the literally exalted distance between the Earth
and God.

The humblest experience of joy confirms that the soul fills the
glory of the skies with its song or the world with its nothingness.
And the same for time: beatitude runs from generation to generation, so that the devout inhabits the unfurled omnitude of space
and history.

Accompanied by joy, experience opens this space—which goes
from there to elsewhere and can go from Earth to God—for the
construction or dilation of the soul, by opening up or piercing a
passage, a threshold, a door, a port through which to reach one of
these exposed places. Experience traverses these places and is
exposed. Between nothing and everything, it launches a space and
a time, like a free and floating branch. Ecstasy expresses an end to
this voyage, the establishment, temporarily stable, or, rather, a distancing from the equilibrium around this exposed point, in its
neighboring regions, a differential of time.

Programmed, the bestial instinct closes in on itself, positioned.
The animal is a being-there. In being exposed through experience,
man enters into time and opens it. The human does not exist without experience.

Let us call soul the kind of space and time that can be expanded
from its natal position toward all exposures. Thus the thorax, the
uterus, the mouth, the stomach, the sexual organs, and the heart
are dilated and fill themselves with wind, with life, with wine, with
songs, with goods, with pleasures, with the other or with recogni-

tion—with hunger, with thirst, with misery and with resentment, also. The scope is enlarged by joy and sorrows. We are sewn from elastic tissues. In being brought up, a third place opens in the body to fill it with others. The body becomes pregnant.

Joy. Having returned to the valley, I still inhabit the summit of the mountain that I scaled last week, I am dilated from here to the top, yes, from way down here to the Very High; my soul, low, haunts, in its variety of times and spaces, the Goûter dome, Mont Blanc, and the glacier of Grands-Mulets. No, I do not remember, but their magnificence, having entered me, remains there: it was certainly necessary that my body grow, just as it once expanded to the dimensions of Mount Everest. *Et exaltavit humiles . . .*

Thus, ever since my most fragile youth, I have erected my tent way up there amid mathematical idealities, and beyond the water amid faraway longitudes. I wander in the world and the back worlds, in bold abstraction, landscapes, cultures and languages, social castes . . . my soul is exposed in learning things, just as it ventured onto the slope of glaciers and still remains there. To open the door, to pierce the partition, is ultimately to expose oneself to death. A life of experiences forges the passage, short or long, sterile or fruitful, from nothingness to death, while passing through indefinitely dilated joy.

There is no humanity without experience, without this exposure that moves toward explosion, no humanity without these dilations.

Suddenly these dilations, right in the middle of the body, are filled with a third, which is me without being me. In being raised, the self is begotten.

Social grandeurs, false, annihilate this distance: superb, the rich and the potentates lay claim to their own sites, their chairs, their goods, their power, their glory, and, in distancing them respectively from these dispersed places, from their emptied riches, and from their overthrown power, God makes them bigger, in fact, or magnifies them . . . *deposuit potentes de sede . . . et divites dimisit inanes* . . . Only then is the distancing reproduced, and only then do they become big again, big through dispersion or inanity, big because deposed, three true measures of grandeur and volume.

Experiencing, with hunger in my chest, my stomach, my uterus, and my heart (*re-cordatus miseri-cordiae,* here, again, a measured breadth), the immense space of my exposed soul, I receive, humble, at the low point of the terrestrial place, the streaming goods from the high point, the nonplace of God, which fill up to the hilt this magnificent distancing that one calls me . . . *esurientes implevit bonis.* The psalm of the Virgin invents the soul as the measure, in grandeur and volume, of this dilation. Ontologically, the soul is large; grandeur, metrically, produces it. The soul is joy, psychologically. Ethically, the inverse, contraction, shrinking, destroys it: mortal sin of pettiness, of pusillanimity.

Knowing neither sense nor direction, our wandering goes from being-there toward exposure, from humility, the veritable essence of the human, toward the absent and high nonplace, our fulfillment, and this movement creates distance and exaltation, our grandeur and our being—an empty or full, miserable or joyous distance. Misery and joy together complete the fundamental experience that we can have of being, of life, of the world, of others and of thought.

This experience makes little reference to a subject place, but above all to that space of which the humble subject only constitutes the lower lip or border and of which the second place, exposed, marks the other extremity: precisely the border of the other. Thus my soul, in the third place, is equivalent to this grandeur, limted only by the local me of the earth, below, and a crowd of others, of all kinds, above.

In these high, exposed places, without which we are nothing—a self without joy—lives God himself, omnivalent, universal, complete appellation whose undefined versions are named, in turn, the Goûter dome, a given ideality, this airport at the end of the world, you whom I love and who loved me, the world whose beauty amazes me and to which I give myself, the object that I observe and that fills me with information, the thought that I develop and the language that rains on me, the sweet crowd of those around whom I gravitate, you, all of you, strangers or intimates . . . there is therefore no man without God, without this God-function, without the creation and the experience of this exposed abyss of which I am nothing but the low riverbank, a local and earthy lip, without this high and wide expandable space that I experience here and now in my thorax, my heart, my stomach, my uterus, my soul . . . without this opening toward the sum of alterity.

The space dilated by learning, the other fills with a being, third, me and not-me, to which, one day, I will not give birth.

In the subject, first person, the others engender a third person, who is finally well *brought up.*

Morning. Darkness. Silence. Waking. Small, already lively gestures. The new force is ready. The bomb primed. Joy offered. What is to be done? Yes, undertake something and in a big way. Go beyond the seas, construct, discover . . . Enthusiasm elicits, at dawn, the return to the world; the world and I have returned to the morning of creation. Omnipotence: everything again becomes possible. Magnificence: this capacity tends toward greatness.

Which? Where, how, and for what? So, at the moment of deciding, while remembering history, which only makes great things from the dead, from the feet to the eyes and from one shoulder to another, my body, made for greatness, mourns for greatness. Present in my body, evident, invading . . . unused.

The body does not form grandeur, does not show it, gives it nothing social or historical, except through crimes and lies; neither the victory that tramples a thousand vanquished, nor the excellence that deposes the cohort of the mediocre.

And, from infallible experience, since my violent, weighty, demanding childhood, grandeur lies in me and dilates. Every day then, it awakens a ready energy, as it has for several decades, to go forth at the first call, attentive watcher, loyal servant, devoted unto dying, but obeying only greatness.

This free, early omnipotence, this immense demand, can be exhausted in a work; but this work only rarely achieves greatness and doubtless anonymously, because it is not a question of me, but of the work that produces and will give birth to me. Thus, the unusable power remains intact, youthful and fresh even in old age. Virginal, to be precise. It sings the *Magnificat.*

Now nothing can make an exception of this experience. Doubtless, everyone, one day at least, experiences this formidable dilation of his being—in explosive volume, strength, and potential—this free break, this unemployed greatness, that remains virginal no matter what one does, the infinite regret of remaining to one side: the infinite possibility of learning.

Why stubbornly refuse to call this vacant intensity, potential world and thought right in the middle of the body, which is like a rose window or a small sun, the soul?

Instruction

Day. Neither the Sun nor the Earth is situated at the center of the world. Formerly, philosophy extolled the Copernican revolution for having chased our planet from the center, but Kepler discovered that the general movement of the stars follows elliptical orbits that together, to be sure, refer to the solar donor of power and light; but each, in addition, refers to a second focus, of which no one ever speaks, as efficacious and necessary as the first, a sort of second black sun. To the white, brilliant, and unique sun correspond several dark foci that can be gathered into a sort of ring-shaped zone that is exposed, I mean to say posed, away from the Sun.

In addition, neither of these two poles is in the middle.

The real center of each orbit lies precisely in a third place, just between these two foci—the shinning globe and the dark point. No, neither the Sun nor the Earth is in the center, but, rather, a third lost zone, of which one speaks even less than one does of these solar partners.

In the same way, a measurable distance separates a second black focus from the sun of knowledge, which, though dark, is at least as active. *Research,* a term in current usage whose Latin root comes from *circle,* as does that of *encyclopedia*—a scholarly word that the learned Rabelais copied out, in Greek, from the former—together bespeak a circular gnoseology, centered solely on one source of light. In speaking of a center of research, language, redundant, rambles and delays, because there exist, to our knowledge, second foci apart from the first that bend the perfect cycles in an eccentric manner. Yes, knowledge functions elliptically, as Kepler already said of the planetary system.

The weak and the simple, poor or illiterate, the whole gentle crowd so derided by the learned that they see it as nothing but the object of their studies, those excluded from canonical knowledge follow the black holes, doubtless because the black holes neither blind nor overwhelm them, or because they sustain them as much as the sun thrills philosophers. Besides, would the scholars themselves recognize the solar moments of powerful knowledge if they were not mixed with long hours of black sun? Is true intuition accompanied by an indispensable weakness? And what does intuition owe to this weakness?

For purposes of clarity, knowledge becomes decentered, like the world, but does so, like the world, through its momentum, the energy of its movement. We do not know what incites us to leave ignorance behind, the motivations and finalities, even less where knowledge is heading. Motivity is divided between the blinding source of light and a second dark point. Nonknowledge borders knowledge and is mixed in with it. Single—concerned with the same world and the same men—research turns, according to its objects, around a center that is equidistant from these two foci.

To measure the constant separation of these two poles, to estimate what the flamboyant star owes to the blind point and the latter to the former, to search for the reasons for such a distance, to evaluate the productivity of the dark zone and even the fecundity of this double and no longer simple command or attractive regulation—Who would lose one without the other?—this is the program of the Third Instruction, given in terms of Kepler's law.

What can be said of new centers? Formerly a poem whose verse or verse fragments were borrowed from various authors was called a *centon*. By extension, this is what we should call any kind of work, literary, historical, musical, or theoretical made from copied-out bits and pieces. Transcribe a single model and you are called a plagiarist, but if you copy one hundred, you are soon awarded a Ph.D. For example, this study of Greek/Latin roots of the word *center* can be reduced to a centon. A word rarely used, in truth, whereas the potpourri it describes occurs frequently.

The Latin language, thus, already knew the word and the practice; these hodgepodges, also called satires, were already composed in that tongue, from which it is evident that laziness is timeless. But before designating such a mixture as chosen morsels to be recited, sung, or cited, *cento* referred to a patched-up piece of cloth, a scrap of composite fabric. Harlequin's coat has returned, the comedian at the center of the stage and of this book.

I regret the eclipse of the French word among the abundance of objects it ought to designate. This word, like its Latin equivalent, goes back to the Greek *kentrôn*, which translates *cento* and *centon* precisely: a poem made of pieces taken from various sources and a patchwork coat, one playing the role of the other's image. But, first and primarily, *kentrôn* designates the goad the laborer formerly used to stimulate a pair of bulls in the harness; the weapon in the belly of a bee or at the back of a scorpion; but also a studded whip, an instrument of torture.

Now the same word designates the instrument of punishment and the one who suffers or merits it—the victim. *Center* thus ends up bespeaking the wretched one, condemned to stirrup leather or to the mortal goad, and describes his place. *Kentrôn* thus translates the center of the circle, the sharp point, the singularity situated in its middle. The very place on the planks where Harlequin undressed. I no longer recall in which village of my childhood the central square was given this name: place des Centons.

All alone, effortlessly, language speaks in several voices and recounts the striptease of the prelude without me. First the coat, a patched-together centon, then the merely additive and composite narrative of shedding successive leaves of clothing or the pages that recount this undressing; witness, also, the Emperor of the Moon in the center become a public laughingstock, his turban-wrapped head soon appearing beneath jeers and whistles; see finally what the Harlequin wears in the center of his center, in the heart of all the folds of his clothes, or beneath all his beneaths: what he is, one and several.

He is the central point where he is, the colorfully patterned reunion, in an indivisible point of intersection, of directions and surrounding worlds. The coat of this vain peacock sparkles with the eyes of those that look at him, blue and black looks, green and nut-brown glances. To him alone, the word *center* speaks of the singular and the multiple simultaneously: the latter, in its obvious spatial sense, of intersection, and the former, in its hidden linguistic roots, of reunion; the two at last, in geometry.

Following the history of the sciences, language recounts that the center of the circle or that the center in general, this pure ideality, far from designating from the outset the calm site where one debates in serene, democratic equality, describes the trace left by the prod, stimulation with a distinct style, but also the stud and the whip of the rake, the site of torture and the place of the ridiculed king: geometry arrives in last place, dragging behind it this past, just as the tail of a black comet drags behind it the shinning nucleus. A Saint Sebastian traversed by arrows, lies, stuck there, pierced, flagellated, behind or beneath the transparency of this pure concept of center whose limpidity hides, better than a screen can, the residues of archaic advanced training. The history of sciences leaves room, upstream from itself, for an anthropology of geometry, which geometry, being pure, forgets.

The second black sun appears, at a distance from the dazzling one; our speculative bedazzlement before the center of the circle obscures the black sun. There is shadow in the neighborhood of this light, and pain beneath this serene concept.

At the center lies the centon; covered with pieces, composed of bits. In this ultimately punctual and almost absent singularity, the entire world is gathered and meets, is often juxtaposed or is sometimes founded.

In the center lies the subject, thrown beneath these pieces, the receiver of information and pain.

Upbringing, instruction, education form this central subject, in the image of the center of the world. Brilliant and somber, the world converges toward him.

Night. To canonize the relations of knowledge and light, of the world and the subject, astronomical imagery, whose splendor runs from Plato to Kant and beyond, rarely takes into account that observers are night owls who do most of their work after sundown.

Not only does knowledge lie away from the center and demand the support of secondary black suns, but the center itself, an almost useless half-place *[mi-lieu]*, is suddenly sown throughout the universe, an immense milieu where the terrestrial, solar, and planetary world is reduced to a district. In the course of long, dark nights, these light and dark regions, mixed together, issuing from thousands of shinning suns and holes said to be black, are observed.

Canonized by the crushing monarchy of the day, our knowledge unjustifiably established the local solar system as a general law. Now, midday signifies nothing more than the small principality of a nearby dwarf star. We receive from far away the light of other suns, sometimes giant, but drowned in shadow.

According to the Keplerian revolution, not only has the sun left the center, but a myriad of suns exists. Absent or almost absent from the first figure, the center is reproduced, multiplied, throughout the whole of the universe—its quasi nothingness is indefinitely sown. The astrophysical revolution has lost count.

Subjects exist everywhere, amid light and shadow.

Translated from space into duration, nostalgia and narcissism, which dream of a subject in the center of everything, begot the strange idea that two analogues of this center exist in time: the beginning and now, the latter continually optimized as the moment when we know the most things best.

Why, in effect, like space, would time also not be sown with an infinity of centers or crowning moments? How many beginnings and ends are truly taking place this minute? Yes, now always begins a new destiny, or, if you want, closes an era or remains gently indifferent. Choose from among these equivalent truths.

As a third between two poles, shining and dark, the center, from nowhere goes everywhere, in space and time, and, from nothing, becomes multiple.

The sun not only gives light, but also power, in its role as an attractor. Since Kepler, each planet is found to be attracted not only by the sun, but also by the other black focus. Now we know of a multiplicity of attractors in various forms that produce chaotic orders.

Research or the encyclopedia of knowledge, once reputed to be round, follows an equivalent history: it already becomes elliptical or has two attractive foci in Auguste Comte—via the hard and social sciences, physics and sociology—before being dispersed today and enjoying several centers or attractors; the form and concept of the old encyclopedia change; one cannot, all the same, call it a *chaopedia!*

This does not mean that laws are forgotten, but that prediction is lowered to a certain unpredictability. This draws sciences and things themselves closer, because no one knows or can predict the invention of laws, even if they remain the height of reason and determinism. In both cases, in the case of knowledge and of the universe, there is history, through this mixture of prediction and unpredictability; inversely, conceiving of history now becomes easy, because the encounter of determined reason with chaos never ceases.

A certain disorder favors synthesis.

Chiaroscuro
The sun loses its sovereignty over knowledge; it is no longer the final end nor the first beginning of knowledge, but is reduced to a

small cone of bright dust issuing from a fissure in the black box of space. Midday only produces an oblique bedazzlement. We cast aside neither our ignorance nor our limitations. Light no longer floods volume, does not occupy space, does not take up all the room, like a god under whose reign nothing will ever be new, but comes to us, like a ray displayed among myriad rays, in spectral, singular colors. Issuing from a sun, each examined, colorfully patterned, tigroid, knotted, zebrine band is furnished with differentiated information. The coat of Harlequin, Emperor of the Moon, also figures this night knowledge.

Beneath the unique and total sun shone the unity of knowledge. At dawn, its light extinguishes the innumerable multiplicity of different stars. All quiet since the Eastern front. Nothing new since this fire has illuminated us, since the age of Enlightenment: since this Greek Sun, a single God, and classical science, since Plato, the wisdom of Solomon, Louis XIV, and the Aufklärung, this daylight knowledge had lost time. None of these names, none of these so-called new eras ever changed the regime, always the same, of light, unique and atemporal.

Here is something new. No longer naively opposed to the day, like ignorance to knowledge—what wonderful luck nycthemeral rhythm is for the simple and cruel divisions of error and truth, of science and dreams, of obscurantism and progress!—but sown with colors and black, night is the sum of the very days of knowing. Thus harlequin and chromatic, the third instruction, like the preceding ones, comes from night owls in observatories of space that mix the day with night, which, in turn, integrates the days of galaxies with the night of black holes; this mixture engenders a third light.

We have left behind the Platonic Good, the Age of Enlightenment, the exclusive victory of classical science, the unitary history of our fathers. Never did triumphant religions, politics in its hour of glory, science that thought it had reached its apogee whereas it was barely beginning, or history without falsification tolerate images of such discretion or grace, nor the mixture from which time is born.

This is the age of glimmers. Knowledge illuminates the place. Trembling. Colored. Fragile. Mixed. Unstable. Circumstantial.

Shadowy. Encumbered. In the ray of clarity, colorfully patterned, saturated with dust, dance the atoms. The Sun King sees his laurels in ashes. Far from illuminating the universal, knowledge blinks beneath the sheer weight of dust motes. This is the age of local brightness and eclipses, the age of scintillation. Perhaps we now prefer the chromaticism of light to its unity, its speed to its clarity?

But again where, in third instruction, does this necessary shadow so mixed with light come from, then?

From pain, like the shadow that hid the center?

The Third Place

Each ellipse shows a center and two foci: here is a third, a group of three. But what is one calling third there? A third place, a third man, the third person?

In a third place in the middle of the others, the third person can find himself in a delicate and ambiguous position, if he is not—or is too—involved. Bearer, for example, of good or bad news, interpreter, he profits, sometimes immensely, from a situation that, often, is also reversed, and he can then be unmercifully chased, excluded like a parasite. Scrounger or messenger, too well or very badly placed, the third, in the center, between the two others, suffers or abuses. Expelled for interfering, intercepting, getting too involved.

The one who took up too much room loses his place.

Of two people who contradict each other, one must be right and the other wrong: there is no third possible; it is said, the Third is excluded; or better yet: there is no middle [*milieu*]. Truly? Remarkably, the French language defines this word *milieu* as a point or an almost absent thread, as a plane or a variety with no thickness or dimension, and yet, all of a sudden, as the totality of the volume where we live: our environment. New reversal: from the half-place [*mi-lieu*], a small excluded locality, insignificant, ready to vanish, to the milieu [*milieu*], like a universe around us.

What had no more room takes up all of it.

Just as a vibrating string sounds, the third does not cease oscillating—scintillating—between good and bad news, profit and derision, indifference and interest, information and pain, death and life, birth and expulsion, everything and nothing, zero and infinity, the point of which one never speaks, between the two foci, the solar and the black, and the universe that it sows.

In the fifth century B.C., some anonymous Greek sages discovered, in geometry, the apagogic proof, that is, proof through the absurd. In measuring the diagonal of a square having sides of length one, they became apprised that the length of the diagonal could be expressed neither by an even nor an odd number. From this contradiction, the third should have been excluded. But if that were the case, the said diagonal wouldn't exist; well, here it is, in relief, decorating, precisely, the mid-place *[mi-lieu]* of the square, which it separates in two without a middle *[milieu]* imposing itself on intuition. It exists then, but it is ineffable. It was called inexpressible, irrational, other. Now, an innumerable multiplicity of such others appeared suddenly in numbers and graphs: the algebra of real numbers, the true kind; great mathematics had just been born.

It was born from the excluded third, from this impossible situation: neither this nor its opposite; from this inexpressible source, from the absurd that the diagonal of the square drives us to the brink of, neither even nor odd, to the absence of a middle between these two impossibilities of naming it. From then on, the discovery of real numbers, spurting like a geyser from this absent fault line, insists that all other known numbers, at least in those days, be reduced to limit cases of this new form, absurd mid-place at first, thus worthless, then invading, an almost complete milieu. Soon one will not find anything but this third, as soon as its exclusion is pronounced. It was nothing, see how it becomes everything—or almost. Absurd *[absurde]* means deaf *[sourd]:* The hubbub that Genesis says precedes creation, does it come from such a silence?

Whoever took up too much room loses his place; who had none takes everything; nothing can become everything, which can be drowned in nothingness. The law of transformation through unpredictable bifurcations.

The *parasite,* a small animal, follows this law; in multiplying to change levels, it produces epidemics that put giant groups of large animals to death, but, at the same time, exposes itself to disappearance. Hermes himself reproduces it, in his usual role of intermediary from which one expects that he will transmit messages like a

transparent, thus worthless, windowpane, but who actually transforms the whole cultural landscape with each bit of information, a
middle becoming a milieu: odious and indispensable animal and
god, good and bad angels together, mediators, effectors of change.

Thus expressed, the said law, a lesson of ancient books, governs
real transformations and begettings. Can this law produce time,
not the time of clocks, but ours, that of our souls, of what we know,
that of things and of history?

Of history, for example? Those who belonged neither to the
nobility nor to the clergy were grouped by the Old Regime in a
third class: the third estate. The third estate was nothing, not
involved, often excluded, and it wanted to become something, with
the success now known to us. Today, in the same way, carried by its
giant demographic growth and risking economic death, the Third
World demands to develop. What will happen to it?

In knowledge and instruction, a third place also exists, a worthless position today between two others: on the one hand, the hard
sciences, formal, objective, powerful; on the other, what one calls
culture, dying. Whence the begetting of a third man; the third-
instructed, who was nothing, emerges today, becomes something
and grows. He is born in this book, and, as his father, I wish him a
long life.

Here is an apologue that locates the two places: do you dream of
someday obtaining the Nobel prize in medicine, economics, or the
physical sciences? Then work in a rich English-language university.
But, for literature, in view of the same award, you are better off writing and living in the Third World. This triple geographic distance
of fortune and speciality shows the level of derision to which the
esteem once accorded to the humanities has fallen: cultures of misery, misery of culture.

Can one delay the inevitable confrontation of the North—
happy, knowing, blessed—and the wretched South by means of the
invention of this third-instructed culture? It is at once a question of
wisdom, in the intellectual sphere, of justice, in economic matters,
of the protection of the Earth, as well as of peace, our supreme
good.

Epistemology and pedagogy meet, just as they did before, in the
center, in exclusion, pain, violence, and poverty; the problem of
evil crosses knowledge. See the shadow.

As Kepler taught us, we believe that at the common center of the
world the universal sun of knowledge and reason shines, but that
the shadow is dispersed in the second foci of diverse planets; it
occurs to me today to think, on the contrary, that the problem of
evil is involuted in the common center of all cultures, and that a
thousand suns of diverse knowledges scintillate amid the common
milieu of this painful, universal shadow.

I suffer: that has been said everywhere, always; we think: this cog-
ito, specialized, concerns only rare communities.

We have to educate ourselves in the third place between these
two foci.

The Third Man

The third person haunts our words and our languages. Let's enter
into a dialogue, chat, so that the god Hermes will circulate among
us anew, let us communicate then: *I* converse with *you, you* address
us, the linguistic roof of our belonging shelters the first and second
person, understood as singular or plural. So well-defined and
closed that we remain deaf to everything except what happens in
this belonging, this sphere includes the same and the other in
excluding the absent, worthless, or ridiculous thirds.

In the course of dialogue, *he* or *she, that, they,* outsiders, designate the exclusion or the exterior of the closed group of our conversation, the state of not belonging to our communication, therefore a third place, plus, to be accurate, the one that, the ones or
those, without whom, without which or with whom and of which we
speak, the third included and excluded.

These grammatical third persons, generally issuing from pro-
nouns or *demonstrative* adjectives, are thus exactly, *demonstratively,*
this third whose preceding logical, geometric, and social avatars we
already know. We pass our arms through the windows of belonging,
to indicate or point at these third persons, outside.

Now, for these thirds, again, the same iron law describes the
same transformation: nothing can become everything, which can
drown in nothingness. The third person, excluded, badly placed
on the edge of the mid-place, rarely bears the name of a person,
because he borrows his own name from a demonstrative, but can
become the milieu of everything and, in particular, of us—we who

are given over to language, that objective and intersubjective milieu in which our tongues have always been immersed. Besides, and still, this relation of nothing to everything offers up the secret of begetting, of becoming and of time.

The figures of the third excluded or the third person from now on no longer traverse the lacunary space of the preceding examples, which seem to have become various categories by chance, but, on the contrary, fill, saturate the ontological universe. In the same way, in this book, the portrait of the third-instructed, me in first person, you, completely other, in second, suddenly abound and engender one, two, ten models, as many thirds as one could want.

Teaching is this sowing.

Here then is the third person become the totality of the social collective that surrounds those who talk of him; in this case, he is named: *one* or *each* or *all* or *the others.* Either pregnance or expulsion. In second place, the third person becomes the totality of objects or of objectivity in general: surrounding us, without us, the *this* or *that* that we point at. Thirdly, the world as such or the physical world—impersonal, accurately denominated: *it* rains, *it* thunders, *it* hails, *it* snows; inclement weather *[les intempéries]* designates, again and profoundly, the temporal operator. Thirdly, Being itself: the French expression for being there, there is *[il y a],* translates, word for word, and using, precisely, the third person and its locative case, the German *dasein.* Finally, morality: *it* is necessary *[il faut],* third imperative as impersonal as the objective *it* rains.

The third person thus indexes the full circuit or the synthesis of knowledge and its objects. Who, today, would have even dreamed of such a union? Of holding the threads of such a totality in one hand?

The Third and its vibrant law of exclusion and inclusion thus found the sciences, both the hard sciences and the humanities *[sciences humaines],* the first establishing themselves on rigorous proof alone, founded on the principle of the excluded third (we see, in the evidence and, doubtless, for the first time, how easily one passes from the linguistic demonstrative, pronoun and adjective, simple gesture of the extended index finger that indicates the outside, threatens or admires it—the Latin *iste* of derision becomes the *ille* of glory—to the proof that rigorously concludes, through the well-regulated functioning of exclusion), and the second, founded on global becoming and local exclusion, which defines or designates, first of all, a given individual, then, suddenly, the totality of social inclusion; it is a question, in both cases, of the same foundation, and furthermore, they found each other. From social and human exclusion, one moves to the excluded third who, in turn, renders collective conduct and all its consequences absolute and rigorous. Here at last we discover a Northwest passage where one is born in both senses, where beginnings are substituted for each other and beget each other.

Metaphysically, the Third and its law found physics, while linking it to proof, by giving nature its general objectivity, as well as by making natural phenomena function outside the intention of those concerned with, and within the purview of, discourse. They found the ontology of being itself, but, on top of that, time and history, by furnishing the operator of transformations. Finally, they found morality by discovering a law of conduct that references no particular will, that is outside the sphere of communication.

Thus the third person provides a foundation for the whole of the external real, for objectivity in its totality, unique and universal, outside any first- or second-person subject. Here, outside all *logos,* the reason of realism, an unprovable philosophy without this third person, which is now, thanks to it, more than provable, since it is present at the root of every proof.

This is the goal and the end of the philosophy of communication brought by the message of Hermes, an outsider or third between the first and second person, circulating among their relations: neither the philosophy of communication nor its god can do without what is neither philosophy nor god.

To Instruct or Beget

Whence knowledge, experience, and instruction. Formerly, the slave who took the noble child to school was called a pedagogue. Hermes also went along, sometimes, as a guide. The little one leaves the family home; departure—second birth. All learning demands this voyage with the other toward alterity. During this passage, lots of things change.

You must love the language that transforms the slave into the master himself; and thus the trip into school itself; and that trans-

forms this emigration into instruction. The slave knows the outside, the exterior, exclusion, what it is to emigrate; stronger and
adult, he catches up a bit with the more fortunate child, establishing a temporary equality that renders communication possible. In
the same way, wandering in the forest, Snow White encountered
old dwarfs: ancestors, since they were old, but children in size, a
quasi equality that permits her to remain protected while becoming a protector, still a child, already mature; mother, quickly, and
child, still. She will thus be reborn, from herself, from them, from
the forest, in her self and otherwise, a daughter who is mother of
herself. There is no teaching without this self-begetting. Thus,
from above, the rich child speaks to the poor adult slave who
answers, from his greater stature; maybe, all of a sudden, they will
take each other's hands, in the wind and beneath the rain, forced
to shelter a moment beneath the foliage of the beech tree, above
which the third person thunders: it is snowing, it is cold. Other and
experiencing alterity painfully, the slave is familiar with the exterior, has lived outside.

Thus the world enters the body and the soul of the greenhorn:
impersonal time and also the strangeness of the excluded, *iste,* the
derided slave, and soon that of the master, *ille,* still far away, at the
end of the voyage. Before arriving, he is no longer the same,
reborn. The first person becomes the third person before entering
the school door.

Learning consists of such crossbreeding. Strange and original,
already a mixture of the genes of his father and mother, the child
evolves only through new crossings; all pedagogy takes up the
begetting and birthing of a child anew: born left-handed, he learns
to use his right hand, remains left-handed, is reborn right-handed,
at the confluence of both directions; born Gascon, he remains and
becomes French, in fact a half-breed; French, he travels and
becomes Spanish, Italian, English, or German; if he marries and
learns their culture and their language, he is a quadroon, octaroon, soul and body combined. His mind resembles Harlequin's
iridescent coat.

This holds for bringing up bodies as much as it does for instruct-
ing. The half-breed, here, is called the third-instructed. Scientific
by nature, attracted by the solar focus, he enters culture. The com-
monality of reason sends the different black holes back to their cul-

tural particularities. Now, by a strange symmetry, the problem of evil—injustice, suffering, violence, and death—culturally universal, occupies the whole zone of the shadowy focus, from which one learns to see clear reasons like so many variable and separated rational solutions. Thus the mind changes its medley of colors.

Finally, this holds for behavior and wisdom, for education. Already other, the companion leads to an encounter with a second person—a hard and demanding experience, beneath the wind and the stars—from which the self begets in itself, without abandoning its own person or its unity, a third person.

Love the one who begets spirit in you.

The Third Person

Present throughout the universe, but absent to the point that no one can find him there (since he hides so much), everything then and nothing, nothing but everything, God comprises, in addition, the law of incarnation that wants everything, in the world and time and history, to become nothing, a humble son of a carpenter born in a miserable stable, condemned to death and crucified as a slave, encountering, marrying, assuming the problem of evil, finally becomes everything once again, seated, resurrected, at the right hand of his Father, that is, the second person; the third person, the Holy Spirit,[1] comes from the first two.

One pictures the Father, omniscient, seated on the throne of power and glory, stable. In the end, he will have worked for a week. Since then, he has been enjoying rest. The Son descends to the earth, and, lower still, toward Hell, finally to be resurrected, then, at the Ascension, returns to the Heavens where he will come to judge, on the last day, the living and the dead. From God who is incarnated, the two movements achieve, in the end, an equilibrium: not solely static, but compensated by redemption or expiation. Second stability: invariance through variations, including, in passing, a tragic solution to the problem of evil. Here is the shadow and the light, suffering and omniscience.

The third person of the Trinity, the Holy Spirit, takes the form of a bird, a dove, sometimes the appearance of a tongue of fire or an

1. In French, *esprit* means both mind and spirit.—TRANS.

impetuous breath: *it* is windy, *it* thunders, *it* is lightening. Breeze, noise, or flame, the Holy Spirit is propagated where and when he wants, falls on us, here, there, never or tomorrow, suddenly, like inclement weather, lightning that splits the sky or rain . . . and the winged creatures are borne up only by the turbulences that form beneath their wings. Neither in flight nor through the turbulent winds can traces of equilibrium, stability, or compensation be found. The sowing of the spirit or mind depends on the heat and the air, thus on the weather *[temps]*, which is rather aleatory, and not on measured, regular time *[temps]*: it penetrates the world in whirlwinds. Nothing, everything; everything, nothing. A miniscule morsel of language inside a closed room, all the languages of the world known in the public square, here, again, the vibrant law, that of the Pentecost.

Neither wind, nor fire, nor birds in flight know rest. The third person comes from two others, it happens through procession. This last word describes a step forward, like a raised foot, which is exposed. The Holy Spirit is exposed outside of the Father and the Son, without leaving their unity. No text says that this procession stops, that this launched step comes to rest somewhere: whence the figures of the wing and flight, which never, in volatile fluids, find definite supports. Since, definitely, the prop always gives way, one must always begin again to support oneself on what will always give way. The Holy Spirit thus proceeds, absolutely speaking: it leaves stabilities forever, including those of the balanced movement of circular history, to risk itself in the unstable motivity of deviations from equilibrium. That means that it never stops being exposed. It evolves and travels. Whence its eccentration, outside the stabilities of the first two persons; whence knowledge, whence time. Whence learning.

This real time of wind and fire, of elements and climate, that of the spirit/mind, is equal to that of being brought up, of instruction, of unexpected intelligence and constant advice, of transformations with no return, of languages and sciences, of travels, of inventions and travails, of improbable peace alongside vengeance, of prescription, of unexpected combinations, of alliances . . . Between the two stable persons in their infinite conversation, between omniscience and exposure to evil—one focus shining, the other burning—lies the chaotic time of the spirit, third person.

Conversely, the third man who is born in me, in the course of learning, is spirit.

The time of history combines a circular, physical, and legal time, that of the use of days of the calendar by incarnated works, with the erratic, unpredictable time of the spirit, in proportion or irregular reason in its solution. History also proceeds from spirit.

The world certainly proceeds from these two persons, here is objective creation and redemption or re-creation through expiation, but because the spirit also comes from them, it happens that the real world is the third person, as has been shown, or the mind itself—or that the mind is the world itself or the whole of the objective, which is why the objective can be known, so that finally together they are time, beautiful things that I not only wanted to prove, but that are born at the same time as the proof.

Third person, the known is constructed in the same way that the knower is instructed.

The Third Woman

Scholars first used the word *phenomenology* in celestial mechanics to describe the movements of the planets, their appearance and their reason, then in general physics, before philosophy began to use it for the avatars of the mind or the recognition of stabilities immersed in voluble profiles. Translating this Greek and learned vocabulary vernacularly, one can say "the appearance speaks," a phrase sometimes mumbled, unknowingly, by those placed outside of knowledge. Solar, the first expression, blind, the second, to arrive at the same meaning. Here is a second focus.

In a dark grotto in Lourdes, the Virgin Mary appeared to an illiterate shepherdess to speak of her immaculate conception, as if it were a question of her own procession. The whole pious and naive scene: Anne, the mother, absent, evoked; Mary, daughter and mother, arrived, half-present, speaking, and Bernadette, daughter, silent, visible, of flesh and blood, present there, an ignorant peasant, thus constituting a new feminine Trinity, at the very least unexpected in a culture where the gods or God, shining like suns, were begotten in or proceeded from the masculine; women, finally, proceeding from themselves.

Dark holes of the earth and simple folk that mark a distance from knowledge, in the material of the world and in the soul of men. Yes, myth—can this be said?—lives always and constantly at a distance from science and even the major theological institutions; and the rationalists laugh. Did the Greek Sophists deride the text of *The Republic* as much for the page where Plato evokes the myth of Gyges, another shepherd in ecstasy in a similar cave? Plato granted himself the right to speak of the Sun, beyond geometry and the dialectic, but his text also speaks of the Lydian peasant in his dark grotto. His pedagogy either produces with two foci or consents to an eccentration that we reject, though he thinks before, and we write after, the Keplerian revolution.

We tolerate anthropology, but on condition that it be left to others, to the poor of the Third and Fourth worlds, to those who remain the objects of our knowledge.

Yes, in Lourdes and today in Yugoslavia apparitions speak to shepherds or ignorant children, in caves: a phenomenology of which we ourselves dare not speak. Yet the learned word and the popular phrase, one coming from the blinding solar focus and the other from the black hole, speak of one and the same thing: that appearances, gathered together, seem to speak.

Of the two locutions, quickly name the most attractive and the clearest.

The masculine procession of the Spirit imitates begetting, just like female conception, virginal or immaculate; here are good anthropological models of education, of the production by the other in myself of a third, word or spirit.

In myself spirit is virginally conceived or proceeds.

The Third-Instructed: Ancestors
Third in spirit or language, the sowing of scientific knowledge in narrative or in meditations has a long, illustrious tradition. From Rabelais to Valéry, passing through Molière, Voltaire, or Balzac, ten writers have more or less mastered the science of their time. Science illuminates, fortifies their work, and their work, in turn, illuminates and reinforces science. The shadows and forces come together from two sources that beget the work. The division that

distinguishes the cultivated ignoramus from the uncultured but instructed, in whom the night follows or is juxtaposed to the day, appeared only recently.

The most obvious case of a distribution comparable to that of the heavens concerns an identical body—same author, same invention in domains separated only by our narrowness. Pascal left only one work and, as an ambidextrous person or rather a completed body, wrote it with two hands: *Triangle arithmetique* [Arithmetic triangle] and *Mémorial, Coniques* [Essay on conics] and *Provinciales* [Provincial letters], *Roulette* and *Pensées* together pursue their common quest, precisely that of the center, inaccessible in this infinite world, but which supernatural space causes to appear. Thus Leibniz, Diderot, Goethe, or Robert Musil, whom only our borders present as monstrous exceptions, left behind them a thousand third-instructed texts: metaphysical mechanism, the first writes, while the second recounts determinism on horseback, following its loves and affinities (the latter a word used just as much in mechanics or the geometry of ellipses as in the chemistry emerging at the time), and the last one predicts the probabilities of a meteorology of history. Complete bodies of works.

How can one be surprised that bodies gifted with this completeness would have been seized with the passion of pedagogy? Those who loved their own begetting like to beget. Models of models, Plato, Aristotle, Montaigne, or Rabelais sow their culture with all the knowledge of the time, to model, with this combination, the man to come. Doubtless the educative couple Meno-Socrates, young Telemachus and old Nestor, ignorant and learned, forms the double body of instruction; does one always know what the second owes to the first?

An expert in traditional knowledge whitened by time, the old Egyptian priest of the *Timaeus* treats the Greeks like children; in this I read the perpetual youth of the sciences, their methodical manner of harvesting young shoots. Pedagogy knows the tight knot of these two times. In the usual direction of its flow, from the old to the young, the humanities, archaic, are transmitted; one must get older to understand their wisdom. In exactly the opposite direction, from children to mature adults, the hard sciences make their crossing. Homer played the grandfather from the rosy-fingered dawn of the third millennium, whereas Theaetetus, Pascal, Abel or

Evariste Galois, child inventors of theorems, always died in the flower of their youth. The forefathers with blurry eyes blindly pass on the contents of culture, almost always obscure, while from downstream come the clear messages issued from bright-eyed youth. Questioningly, I teach my granddaughters a bonhomie whose nobility still governs me, but, in return, they teach me the recent developments and achievements of science and technology. One kind of knowledge, maturing, is like good wine, whereas the second kind, new, unceasingly becomes greener. Youthful Nobel Prize winners in science next to patriarchs decorated for literature.

From which one must learn, at the same time, what one understands and what one doesn't understand: in the first case, duration disappears, whereas in the second it is produced. The dark projects a time that light shelters, chiaroscuro makes time itself. Children, learn Homer and La Fontaine by heart; inaccessible at your age, they will slowly mature in the center of your body; and learn mathematics clearly.

These two inverse vectors of time and intelligence would distance forever the two bodies of the couple from all teaching, each ignorant of the other, unless the real whirlwind of time or the turbulences of the mind are outlined. The vector of life increases, that of entropy decreases. At the heart of this turbulence, finally adult, where time is knotted, climbs, falls, and seems to stop—one would say a galaxy—the third-instructed projects the naive time of science, in front, and, behind, the experiences of culture, but, behind, unceasingly annuls time by short-circuiting scientific distinction, and constitutes, in front, the long time of humanity through the slow digestion of traditional contents. Adult: young-old with the balanced benefit of both ages.

Will we finally beget the age of reason?

In another median case, doubtless the most frequent, the author produces with one hand while, with the other, he simply gathers information: Zola tells the story of the Rougon-Macquart family and, in so doing, teaches the genetics of his time; but, contrary to expectation, he authentically invents the physical conditions in which the problems of reproduction are posed. The flame carried by the discoverer strides across the fire-breaks. As a novelist, he sings the epic *[geste]* of a tribe and the tribulations of its members, but, in following in the tracks of the elements of the genome, he mimics the exact gesture *[geste]* of the scientists who will describe them.

Even if specialities are divided, the inventive remains undivided. In the furnace of the Souléiade, Doctor Pascal, geneticist, slips into thermodynamics, without Zola ever having left the narrative. Literature speaks science, which reencounters narrative, which, suddenly, anticipates science. Here, live, is the process of begetting.

This middle case thus returns to the first in lightning fashion so that knowledge is never cut up into crystalline continents, strongly defined solids, but is like a group of oceans, viscous and always churning: ten hot or cold currents traverse them and produce gigantic maelstroms. No history of science or history in general, no instruction is possible, no transformation without this fluid whirlpool.

With the pen, at the beginning, in his best hand, Zola learns bit by bit to write with the other. He crosses the river; without realizing it, he begets in himself an unknown scientist.

The most difficult case, at the end of this road, but the one that is most interesting, difficult to spot, rare, shattering, leads the writer to anticipate. I am not talking about recent narratives that have been catalogued under this heading, which are often mediocre, but of sudden intuitions present and hidden, lost even, in pages whose message seems to speak in another tone, of lakes of premonition, of pockets of innate knowledge in exquisite literary moments.

Sometimes, without noticing it, a narrative, a story, or a poem adds together various forms of knowledge. I would like to give each of these texts the authentic title of unknown masterpiece *[chef-d'oeuvre inconnu]:* unknowing, rather, because the sciences converge there in a transparency through which the eye passes without seeing anything; just as the colors in a rainbow dissolve in the white limpidity of everyday light, in the same way different forms of knowledge merge in speech that seems banal. Diderot seems to have understood that it was necessary to name such undertakings dreams, when they are intentionally constructed and when they lull to sleep a learned philosopher, an adult, under the watchful eye of a doctor who is a philosopher and a man of learning, also full grown.[2]

2. Diderot's *Le Rêve de D'Alembert* [D'Alembert's dream].—TRANS.

But the poet does not nourish any project of this kind when in turn he nods off, irritated or rocked to sleep by the buzzing of a wasp around his head. Just as *Le Rêve de D'Alembert*, doubtless a fake dream, affected, drawn by design, projects the extrapolation from the exact and recognized curves of the real science of the time, and makes the various colors that the prism of the text displays shine, Verlaine, in a sonnet from *Sagesse* [Wisdom], "L'espoir luit comme un brin de paille dans l'étable" [Hope shines like a wisp of straw in the stable],[3] is unaware of a whole field of knowledge to come, almost asleep, his elbow on the table, in the crushing heat of the hour, during the midday siesta, his feet in cool puddles of water with which the tiled floor is being inundated, but still sees through a chink that makes dust-motes bright. When noon strikes and the light of Plato's sun penetrates the room only parsimoniously, he describes, as if at night, the deep sound of coanesthesia, invading hearing during sleep, and the deep sound of the world parallel to that of the body, the flight of wasps, dust particles that dance, wisps of straw in the stable. What is not yet and hastens to become a dream allows one to observe, in chiaroscuro, an indeterminate chaos whose constant presence accompanies us, hot organism and noisy universe, buzzing multiplicities from which science like life, language like poetry, draw their beginnings. Vague but rigorous intuition of a future knowledge and epistemology.

These are the ancestors or the pedagogues, pinpointed long ago, of the third-instructed.

Here a second begetting is described, which comes from a second eccentricity, from other contents of knowledge, no longer from the hard sciences, but from stories and languages.

The Third-Instructed, Again: The Origin

"If you do not love me, I love you . . ." Who doesn't know how to sing this refrain from Georges Bizet? Everyone has seen *Carmen*, the most frequently staged opera in history. On the other hand,

3. From Book III of *Sagesse*, trans. by C. F. MacIntyre in *Paul Verlaine, Selected Poems* (Berkeley and Los Angeles: University of California Press, 1948), p. 157.—TRANS.

who has read the novella by Prosper Mérimée? Furthermore, who really knows how it begins?

With a monument of erudition. Linguistics meets geography, history, and archaeology . . . and poses precise and subtle questions: who wrote, parallel to the *Guerre des Gaules* [Gallic Wars], the *Guerre d'Espagne* [The Spanish War]? Though he may have been the major actor, Julius Caesar was not, it is said, the author. Who then? A Roman, a Spaniard? And where did the decisive battle of Monda, for example, take place, where the end of the civil wars was decided against the two sons of the great Pompeii? Pedantic even, philology fights against the toponymy of mountainous Andalusia, between Cordoba and Grenada. One must, to understand them, have done one's studies, know how to read the old maps and the Latin *Commentaries*.

Mérimée even announces a learned article on "the Roman Inscriptions at Baena" that will indeed appear in the June issue of *la Revue archéologique* [Archaeological review] in 1844. Nothing further from Gypsy loves and flying skirts. Yes, *Carmen* begins with learning. This time, the notes at the bottom of the page that so disfigure volumes and the numbers or asterisks with which critics mark up the lines move up arrogantly from the final pages, to which they are sometimes relegated, to the very *incipit* of the novella. A foolish upheaval that makes for a poor *captatio benevolentiae*.

There is the good Mérimée at work among books, comparing the texts and the maps, in the library of the duke of Osuna or in that of the Dominicans of Cordoba. Will he remain there, will he get out? Does one meet femmes fatales dancing through the shelves or among the incunabula?

A moral of the story, already? Certainly, one must go to libraries; it is assuredly good to make oneself learned. Study, work, something will always come of it. And after? For there to be an after, I mean some kind of future that goes beyond a copy, leave the library to run in the fresh air; if you remain inside, you will never write anything but books made from books. That knowledge, excellent, contributes to instruction, but the goal of the other kind is something other than itself. Outside, you can try your luck. Which? Return to the beginning of *Carmen*.

Here is Mérimée inside: archaeologist, cartographer, he reads, copies, takes notes, will thus publish the learned article. Two foci: inside, outside. Now here he is, outside: I am leaving, he says, on a trip to clarify my doubts about the site of the battle fought by Julius Caesar, taking, for all my luggage, some shirts and the *Commentaries;* nonetheless some remains of the library follow.

He seems to travel the Andalusian countryside around the banks of the Guadajoz. But I, in turn, have a strong suspicion that this excursion is nothing but an excursus, even more erudite than the notes, given that the descriptions of the plateau of Carchera and the nearby swamps, copy—with all their mistakes and typographical errors—dictionaries, catalogs, Elzeviers.[4] I catch him with his hand in the cookie jar; liar! I, too, know geography, whence I see that you bring the outside inside the inside, with a twist of pedantry: you pretend to recount a walk whereas I can show that you transcribe a manuscript! When will we get to the Gypsies and the dances? When, then, will we move from the article to the novella, which keeps the young girls and the handsome officers from sleeping?

Day. Meanwhile, everything really begins. One could truly say that the erudite one walks and suffers. No, he no longer copies. Burned by the sun, harassed by fatigue, he is dying of thirst—this does not happen amid pages—and soon goes to drink, lying flat on his belly, like Gideon's brave soldiers. To merit writing a true book—here, the Bible—one must leave Egypt and confront the harshness of the desert, with no protection other than the sky and no wall other than the horizon.

But before being able to quench his thirst, Mérimée seeks . . . and finds a little watering hole full of leeches and frogs. This sighting cannot be a mirage. Yes, everything there is deceptive. Faced with a swamp where the vampire-leeches nourish themselves on the books of others, one can deduce that by directing oneself upstream, some brook that feeds the swamp downstream from it will surely lead to the source, which will be purer and free of parasites.

4. The name of a family of printers at Amsterdam, The Hague, Leyden, and Utretcht (1592–1680) famous chiefly for their editions of the classics.—TRANS.

In other words, the archaeologist, the historian, the erudite Latinist, the cartographer, the philologist . . . very commonly seek sources. The horrible mass of books reveals and conceals the river and its origins: I like to say that sources attract the learned because they are free of the learned! If I wanted to pass for a scholar, I would call all of that *Quellenforschung*.

Here then is the voyager en route upstream. The marvelous stupor of discovery: at the foot of a cliff, in a tranquil shaded cirque of sovereign beauty, there is the spring, which lies bubbling in a basin of white sand. Next to it, on the fine and lustrous grass, a man sleeps.

Does Mérimée play the same trick on us as did Livy, who, in going back up toward the foundations of Rome, suddenly discovers, on the same soft hillock, Hercules himself asleep, while the flock that he stole from Geryon after he killed its owner grazes? A robber, a murderer, like him; like him exhausted, or overcome by thirst, next to the source discovered by Mérimée, whether as a historian or as a man dying of thirst, in this paradisiacal place in which the narrow straits through which this stream of water runs widen, Don José keeps a rifle not far from his hand, just as next to the other lay the club, while the horses, along the downstream gorge, answer each other by neighing, nonsensical calls that echo the muffled bellows of Livy's bulls. Strangely, a similar tableau is unfurled upstream, at the beginning of the two, similarly Roman, stories.

Is it an originary scene as close as possible to the origins?

Is Mérimée here really exposed, now, to the sun, to thirst, to the desert, to violence, to destitution, to villains in seedy inns, to betrayals and death, in sum to evil or reality, or, rather, liar still, does he copy, but without telling us, the very father of Roman history? Should one still hesitate? Why draw an analogous landscape, stream and source, at the beginning, traversed by analogous actors, god or bandit, murder and robbery, black sleep and brute beasts, animal voices deprived of meaning? Is it a question of history, of myth, of narrative?

Where can the sources of this scene next to sources be found? At the limits of *Quellenforschung*, it seems that one must think something like self-referentiality: the spring first should come out of itself; one certainly says that it flows from a source. Yet, numerous visits to those of the Garonne, of the Vienne, and other rivers quickly persuade us that the point of origin is reduced to a gathering, where the basin brings together or collects a thousand small inlets of separate waters coming from upstream, glaciers or humid prairies, issuing from ice or rain. Always and everywhere, the origin goes back to a flowing point of some kind of flux, as if on a geometric axis; among these ordinary places, certain ones simply form a dam.

Let us compare the two stories. Robber and murderer, pursued by justice, the Basque bandit has taken the place of the robber-murderer, a substitution with little difference. Hercules awakens and kills Cacus; Don José kills no one when he wakes up.

Though he comes upon him in flagrante delicto or almost in the act of murdering, someone still excuses Hercules: a certain Evandrus, who played, in those days, the role of governor; charged with the pursuit of justice, he seems to judge the hero but just as quickly spares him by recognizing him as divine; Hercules has killed before our very eyes, and, before our very eyes, has his case dismissed. The victim, Cacus, had a bad name . . . As a result, Evandrus makes history branch off toward myth, the judicial toward the religious. Instead of hanging the murderer, we will honor him on the altars. A god in place of a condemned man, another substitution with almost no difference. Mérimée thus treats the banished one with humanity, whereas his guide ran to deliver him to justice; they, the two of them, reconstitute the character of Evandrus so that the two scenes give the men equal treatment.

Thus, here the narrator makes history branch off, as well, by disengaging it from the judicial: Don José will continue to live free for a moment, because the carabineros, tipped off by the guide, will arrive too late to seize him. The whole narrative will be told while he remains free: between his flight, not far from the springs, and his captivity, followed by his execution, in Cordoba.

Here Hercules and Don José are free—born to gypsy life, were they always as free as air?—but free from whom and what? In both cases, from judges, from justice, from decision. Let us forget Latin and the Spanish language and speak Greek for a minute: the two men free themselves from judgment, that is to say from criticism. Near the sources, criticism lays down its arms.

In Livy, the religious and the mythic branch off from the judicial; in Mérimée the literary narrative branches off from critical scholarship: on both occasions, at the same moment, in the same circumstances, and in the same neighborhood of origin. To put it another way, myth is to the judicial what narrative is to criticism; and criticism is to the judicial what myth is to narrative.

Don José speaks before the executioner hangs him; to begin with, Mérimée dons the garb and assumes the gestures of the critic, leads him down and then loses him on the road of erudition; one could almost say that he sows him. He leaves him near the sources and abruptly turns off.

The two stories—mythic, literary—both free themselves from the judicial. How?

For the accused, for the assassin, Evandrus substitutes a god: for the bandit, Mérimée substitutes a hero. At the precise place of the fork in the road, at the moment of judgment, on the balanced scale, at the instant when the decisive knot should be cut, substitution takes place. Hercules and Don José leave the criminal courts to climb onto the altars or the planks of the theater. In the beginning is substitution.

A god and a hero thus appear in place of two gallows birds, at the top of the terraces or the steps, between the veils of the tabernacle or the curtains of the stage. In the beginning is representation. In all representation, someone is substituted for someone else: a ram for Isaac, an actor for the title role, a text for an action. And there we are.

Who operates the substitution? Evandrus in the first case, Mérimée in the second: the writer or the learned man.

In fact, we still do not know Don José's victim: Carmencita, whom he loved, who loved him . . . if you do not love me, I love you, and if I love you, take care . . . Carmencita, this is the one Don José killed. Now, in the myth without love, Evandrus, whose name means "good man," he who turns the strongest into a god and prejudges the weakest to be bad, has for mother—or wife—Carmenta.

Carmen: Carmencita, Carmenta . . . the two stories, upstream from their origin, exceeding the source itself—mother or mistress of the judge, cause of exile—are knotted together in the same name, in the same body, in the same person. Have we arrived at a common source? Yes, *cherchez la femme.*

Evandrus, the son of Hermes, had, it's said, invented writing, or at least had imported it from Arcadia to the banks of the Tiber. As to Carmenta, his wife or mother, ancestor of the Sibylls, she sings magically.

To write, to speak, to sing, to represent, all operations of invocation or enchantment that substitute software for hardware. Or for the arid desert a climate-controlled library . . . for the old guard, the relief guard.

Mérimée, learned, goes back to the source; charmed, he descends from it, reciting. He would have had to pass through a third point.

Night. From the source emerges the Guadajoz, doubtless, or a small tributary of the abundantly flowing Gaudalquivir river. Let's now descend the major river, allowing ourselves to go from upstream downstream, going down, as the sailors say, from the origins to the thread of time and of the story, an interval that measures the length of Don José's freedom . . . now, on the quay on the right bank, at Cordoba, when the sun sets, after the angelus has been rung, women are bathing, naked, and from the top of the river-bank, at dusk, none can distinguish between an old orange hawker and a young and pretty grisette. You would take one for the other. Emerging from this dark scene at the river's edge—has she just come from swimming across?—by the staircase that deserts the quay, suddenly, the young Gypsy with the black skirt arrives, next to the author. Like Aphrodite, she is born from the waves. For whom was this anadyomenous Venus being substituted?

Carmen, dead and invisible beneath the burning sun of the sources, Carmen, right in the middle of the river's course, suddenly, begotten, seated there, visible, in the middle of the night, right next to the author, present, living, fatal, beautiful, powerful, intoxicating, attractive, bad, witch, terrible Carmen. Source of life and cause of death.

Here we are at the enchanted origin of the story, Roman, Spanish, what does it matter? . . . of every story (let's appreciate that this word evokes at once one of the humanities [history] and the telling of a story of no importance), of speaking, of singing, of opera, of writing, of science, and of narrative in general. *Carmen* bespeaks everything at once, like a joker of substitution.

Meaningless neighing and bellowing, horses and bulls . . . magic songs, sorcery, the good and evil eye, a voice in two opposite directions . . . iniquitous or just judgments, delicious and fatal loves, a double direction following the nonsensical noise of the animals . . . a single direction at last for the narrative that begins and for the river that flows . . . See how a body is born, naked, swimming, inaccessible and nevertheless there, from sources at Cordoba, in the waters of the Guadalquivir. Before and outside every law, magician, chimera, selecting the red and black cards, reading the forked lines in the natural writing of the hand, and before language, singer and dancer, *Carmen* all by itself claims this genealogy.

Every chef d'oeuvre recounts the begetting of its own art. Which is why it is so named: chef.

Scholarship and archaeology, history and philology lead, close to a source, to a substitution whose cause, still upstream, is named Carmen; if one allows oneself to descend downstream, there she is nude, bathing in the waters issuing from this source, as if the river had begotten her. From books toward their origin, a waterway serves as the inductive thread, whose flow, followed in the other direction, in no way leads back to the library or the learned article at all! One would say that a flux has branched off. Dead, the learned article begets the living novella.

This begetting also concerns the writer. He is reborn double, scholar and storyteller, third, like this attractive femme fatale, like the murderous but divine hero, like the river whose branches are drawn in the earth.

Here is the double focus. Scholarship or science relinquishes its clairvoyance, and narrative, blind, debuts as night falls. Groping, scholarship leads to a hyperclairvoyance, and literature, brilliant, begins. Who will decide? Could there exist a supplemental clarity in critical scholarship and a darkness in narrative, because criticism discourses on narrative and not the other way round—well, here, narrative speaks of and comes from criticism and abandons it, as if there existed in narrative a clarity that is suited to leaving science to its blindness: extralucid Carmen. What of this alternating chiaroscuro?

Learned ones, do not put notes at the foot of *Carmen*'s pages, because the beginning of the novella has extracted from them the very essence of what they can give; leave the narrative in peace, because it says, better than any scholarship, exactly what scholarship will never know how to say of itself nor of texts nor of men nor of the world.

Drawing bifurcating networks, *Carmen* teaches the third-instructed excellently, as well as a philosophy of creation. If one follows the course of the river or the valley toward the mountain, one encounters as many confluences as one wants. And to descend, one must choose: either to go downstream to the right, on the side of Inscriptions and Belles-Lettres, or to take the left, toward the recounted narrative. But, at a particular moment and even at every point, because the bifurcations abound, the adventure remains a third party, in equilibrium, a flowing origin, between judgments, love and death, scholarship and literature, erudition and storytelling.

The novella describes the crossing of a threshold or a passage-way: science returns to it and the story descends from it. An exact proof that the source lies exactly in passing through the third point; in the peaceful cirque with the fine field and white sand . . . In this place, to which we return today, sleeps the third-instructed.

The lesson of Mérimée will change our life: learned, he leaves and does not leave his library, and, in this hesitation, copies his scholarly article; but, at nightfall, tired of works by experts, he returns to the river's quays, and among the tanners and the workers, finds she who, upstream of the sources, has always inspired, finds what, always, infinitely surpasses the scholarly: the fascinating tale. Like the waterway, the body of the author bifurcates: with his left hand Mérimée begins to write, truly, and forgets scholarship, copied out with his right hand.

He discovers the flowing origin of his narrative, utters the title and develops the ending.

It could be said that literature gets through where expertise sees an obstacle. As if, drowned in the density of meaning, nonknowledge still knew what knowledge, overflowing with information, will never know again. In the same way, if philosophy consisted of clarifying statements and transforming them into an object of debate, it would do double duty with science. Blindly understood, narrative gets through where philosophy repeats and stagnates.

But only philosophy can go deep enough to show that literature goes still deeper than philosophy.

I see that clear knowledge contains a blindness almost as far-reaching as the dark knowledge contained in ignorance is deep. Sometimes one can only understand if one liquidates one's knowledge in the loyal narrative of circumstance. The solutions do not always reside in the place where one looks for them. One must always pay, that is, accept that one must pay off this change of place with some kind of blindness, in order to see better.

Begetting at Dawn

Stinking of the suint of male sheep, splashed with milk curds around cheeses draining on the rack, the dark cave where Cyclops sleeps defends itself from prying eyes; but he sees more and better—he, the hairy and savage giant, because he has only one eye, in the middle, which casts a laser beam. Ulysses' topmen can lie low in the corners all they want, the paws of the monster unearth and carry them, gasping for breath, to his other hole—his bloody mouth.

Who will cauterize this implacable light? Who will close this second hole that overhangs his mouth? A man named Nohbdy. A man who has wandered for such a long time, by sea and outside the islands, that he has lost everything, that his vessels and his sandals, his tunic, his plans, even his own name still forsake him today. He is no longer counted.

The one-eyed, extra-lucid monster, as powerful as the mountain beneath which he sleeps, who can see even in the black box, bears a name that expresses several names at once: Polyphemous. That means: the one who speaks a lot, the one of whom one often speaks, bard, illustrious and fertile in arguments. He counts a lot. All of his glory emanates from his eye. Furthermore, his common name of Cyclops means circular, occupying all space, inescapable. All-discerning beneath the light of his circular eye and taking hold of language with his devouring mouth, he is surrounded by sheep and rams, disciples, admirers, lieutenants, subjects, slaves, loyal porters, their heads bent toward the ground, intelligence forbidden them.

The sole glimmer that emanates from one hole feeds the second, avid, hole.

Nohbdy, the wanderer, has no name; Polyphemous the encyclopedist has one hundred thousand striking or rigorous words at his disposal.

But who then converses unceasingly, sings at banquets, negotiates, harangues, outsmarts, wins, an incontestable expert in languages? Ulysses. And of whom does one speak since the Trojan War? Of him, one hundred times more than of conquerors and cyclopses. Who navigates circularly, visits all the seas and the known lands? The same. Who can never do without companions, rivals, a court? Ulysses.

Who then bears the name of Cyclops Polyphemous? Ulysses himself.

When the navigator cauterizes the giant gaze, in the center, with his pointed sword, he blinds himself. He kills his own true eye, between the two already extinguished eyes: the shadow follows light in the middle of the two foci. He effaces Polyphemous, his own pen name, his beautiful, renowned last name, not in order to adopt another moniker, but to renounce all: here he is, invisible, Nohbdy. He leaves the glory and the power, the fire and the mountain, the bleating lambs, and flees from the den in the belly of a wooly ram, not taken, not seen. Nobody sees him reborn from the black hole of the grotto, by means of an invisible and animal birth.

He abandons total lucidity, circular and complete science, the mastery of language, ferocious domination over men, pompous titles, loses power to gain humility: more than animal, beneath the four-legged animal and with head lowered. Nohbdy. He is, finally, a writer, creator, artist—at the very least on the austere path that leads to this craft.

Hairy, insatiable, nourished on sheep and human flesh, perfidious, vain, uncontrollably dominating, the first double of Ulysses burns beneath the drunkenness of glory, a powerful demigod holding up the mountain, better than Olympic. The new one overthrows this blinded wreck so as to be reborn from the mortal cavern with a second effaced last name: Polyphemous becomes Nohbdy; here is the authentic author, the absent hole of the beautiful work. He no longer counts.

He even put out his middle eye.

Ulysses, then, has just signed *The Odyssey*.

It is said that Homer could not see. What burnt stake, what scathing pen put out his eyes?

Say, who can recognize that the rosy color of dawn caresses like fingers, who, but a clairvoyant blind man?

The Problem of Evil

Broadly speaking, science, legally universal, seems to be opposed to a given culture, comprehensive and rooted, de facto, in a single place. A single shining focus, many dark ones. But, by extension, every man, on Earth, lives his own culture, without which he would not survive; culture is thus, legally, universal, opposed, by an inverse turn, to science, which, divided in such and such specialities, becomes, in fact, comprehensive and local, sometimes incapable of addressing global problems. A single dark focus, many light ones. The earth comprises the whole set of singular localities and science the universe of specialized regions.

Universal, science travels the circle of what used to be called the encyclopedia. Why trace this cycle? Doubtless because of the order and the homogeneity reason is supposed to have. But, at certain moments, a sort of cam bends the perfect orbit where an eccentricity appears, as if the cycle were losing its smooth surface or its purity. Accidents—that of physics, at the moment of Hiroshima, that of biology, today, or that of earth sciences—interrupt optimism. Are they the internal crises of science?

Reason crosses violence, war, illnesses, death, it encounters the problem of evil, which is traditional in philosophy. Scholarly Mérimée, in returning to the origins, discovers, where the sources are located, the murderer of Carmen; the burnt stake enters the eye of Cyclops, thorn of the circle; the black holes are suddenly sown in the starry sky; facing the noonday sun, the second black focus appears. None of the third-instructed texts evoked earlier, from the novels of Zola to Pascal's *Pensées,* misses this crossing, this sudden encounter of science with evil, suffering, injustice, and pain.

What relationships does reason, prejudged as simply luminous, maintain with this problem, which begets shadow?

An originary liaison. Western reason meets death neither in Hiroshima nor on the occasion of major, contemporary technological risks, but encounters it as long ago as earthly paradise; the tree of knowledge or science induces our first parents to an original sin that has become transhistoric, since the Semitic dawn of our history, which, beneath conjoining skies, is born of Egyptian pyramids, tombs; of the Trojan War, carnage; and of Greek tragedies, violence and expulsion. Against the grain of Hindus and soon of

Arabs, of all our neighbors, near or far, who also pose this question but give it a whole other solution, the West begins at the same time as the problem of evil and wages against it a consubstantial dialogue or combat, so that the tragic founds the West's history, its reason, and the history of its reason.

Reason does not introduce evil, but excludes it. Western science is born of this exclusion. It emerges from the tragic. Its fundamental categories come from it: purity, abstraction, rigor, excluded third . . . Repetitive, its history recounts trials of exclusion and badly defined debates with religion and law, both of which fight against the problem of evil.

It is modeled on a bright sun that purges itself of every shadow, but at the same time it is modeled on the second, black, sun. Yes, reason attains the universal, but, face to face with it, there exists a cultural universal induced by the problem of evil. We are instructed-thirds from the start, in our very foundations.

For better or worse, in this question science quickly takes the place of God or substitutes itself for him. We used to accuse the latter, all powerful and omniscient, of producing suffering and pain. Leibniz's *Theodicy* even made God appear at the fundamental trial of human destiny. But from now on, we only know and are only effective by means of our science. In science or by science, then, the noncircular universal of action and thought encounters, today, as it did at the origin, the scandal of evil.

And, there, it finds culture, before any judgment. Nothing, in science, helps us, in effect, to withstand finitude, nor to conceive of the death of children, the injustice that strikes innocents, the permanent triumph of violent men, the fugitive pleasures of love, nor the strangeness of suffering. . . whereas this was the contribution of cultures whose local rootedness made wisdom enter, easily or with difficulty, singular flesh.

Neither Leibniz nor his successors accepted this Keplerian revolution that consists of placing two foci in charge of knowledge and of the world—two universal suns, reason and pain.

Science wanders, culture takes root. The former does not know single places, but intelligible spaces; it gathers and in consequence travels. It turns. Prosper Mérimée seeks the local truth of bookish information and abandoned works of art. Universal science scours the countryside in quest of sources, of roots, of its foundation.

Oh marvel, here is the paradisiacal place where green grass attracts the sleep of the wanderer and the grazing of the horse, where the fresh fountain will stanch thirst, where beauty favors rest. Finally, the way station. No, the guide, nervous, scents danger, because a man already occupies this place. All the places are always already occupied; did not science begin its wandering for this reason alone, because men, dogs, or armies on the threshold of war always already occupied possible paradises? In fact, this man, right here, sleeps not far from his blunderbuss, a redoutable old shotgun. In the paradise lost of springs and green grass, universal knowledge meets singular evil, injustice, disillusioned loves, violence, murder, hunger.

At the site of the cam where the singular relays the smooth and universal cycle, local pain cries its narrative. Literature has cried misery and suffering since its birth. Science has not yet learned the language of this sob. In this tragic place begins the reason of the third-instructed.

Suffering and misfortune, pain, injustice, and hunger are found at the point where the global touches the local, the universal the singular, science culture, power weakness, knowledge blindness, or God himself his incarnation.

The general watches the battle from afar, through field glasses, and thus does not often die in it; the learned describe or take care of pain, far from complaining of it. Neither the global nor the universal suffer, and, if science and thought refer to collective or formal subjects, only the local undergoes evil. Thrown under, the subject undergoes. Here finally is why he bears that name.

Whence two cogitos. We think and know. I suffer.

Science meets culture when science is incarnated and encounters or produces pain, evil, and poverty. That moment never ends, because it bears the world and history.

First focus: universal and clear scientific reason, a scintillating sun. Second focus, burning: each singular incarnated individual suffering and dying of the harshness of men, *ecce homo*. Philosophy—a third person, third-instructed, proceeding from or begotten by rational universality and painful singularity, painful universality and rational singularity, a spirit that, simultaneously, makes or follows the legal eccentricity of the world and is sown, multiplied, in the universe—avoids neither the center nor the periphery. This is the secret of knowledge: it functions like the world.

We know through the pathetic and through reason, which are inseparable, both universals, one in the focus of science and the other in that of cultures; we think because I suffer and because that is.

Thus at its height the universal attains the singular, here or there, this hero or that example; the summit of abstraction is read and lived in the landscape, that of knowledge lies in the concrete; narrative is the height of criticism or of theory; monotheism reaches its peak in the regime of the mind and the life of the incarnated; the height of science lies in the knowledge of weakness and of fragility.

Whence the idea, a new one, of a cycle of instruction suitable for relaying the human sciences that are expiring because they no longer go forward and no longer go forward because they no longer train anyone and because one can no longer be educated without the hard sciences, without the history of science, of technology, on the one hand, and, on the other, without law or philosophy, without the history of religions or literatures. In short, in relativity and without the reason of both universal foci.

The third-instructed owes his upbringing, his instruction, and his education—in all, his engendering—to reason, a brilliant sun that commands scientific knowledge as much as the second reason, *the same one certainly,* but burning in the second focus, which comes not only from what we think, but from what we suffer. This latter reason cannot be learned without cultures, myths, arts, religions, tales, and contracts.

The social sciences are dying from having forgotten the two fundamental modes of reason, that of the sciences and that of law, the one that comes to us from thought and the one, also universal, that the problem of evil—injustice, pain, hunger, poverty, suffering, and death—inspires in us and that has produced artists, judges, comforters, and gods.

There is only one authentic reason. It illuminates and mobilizes through two forms: without the first, bright, the second would be irrational, but without the second, hot, the first would be unreasonable.

At an equal distance from each, the third-instructed is engendered by science and pity.

War by Theses

Words. Pain, ineffable, surpasses the expressible. Let us avoid saying that we cannot say: the inexpressible, a complete cliché.

The return to the raw given, a singular landscape, through the abandonment of language characterizes either feigned naïveté or true stupidity. In effect, supple, sly, labile, omnipresent, language takes revenge by outstripping the pathetic or vain idiot who, all while claiming to surpass language, repeats the same hackneyed words rather badly. Let us be careful not to confuse the ineffable with a lack of vocabulary: every bank surpasses in opulence the thin wads of money deposited each week by each individual, the vineyards of France promise better vintage than my dark cellar, the sun heats a larger space than our three lumps of coal.

Very dear, more than costly, exorbitant, true naïveté, on the contrary, crowns the long patience of a writer. Beyond the abandonment of his own speech, he has for a long time set up his desk right inside the dictionary. The richer his language, the more trustworthy his work. Just as to speak honestly of the sea, one must have rubbed against its surface in every sense, to speak in one's language it is useful to have made the rounds of it. The writer does not attain style until after such preliminary traversals, in the same way that a philosopher arrives at thought after long journeys in the country of the encyclopedia. No economy, even a theoretical one, can do without this learning. The thinker must begin by learning everything, but because he thinks in his language, he must also become a writer and in order to do so traverse its capacity in every direction. Just as the sailor does not become one unless he has felt his hammock rocked by all the oceans formed or not by local seas, the thinker tests thought by bathing in regional knowledge, just as he also tests his language by not being repulsed by the notion of writing the language of the tactician, the vagrant, the carpenter, the monk, the scholar. In writing amorous, painterly or musical, technical language, he flips through the pages of encyclopedias and dictionaries, surpasses science and narratives. Yes, metaphysics arrives after physics, philosophy begins beyond disciplines and literatures: not only sciences, hard or soft, exact or inexact, rigorous and fluid, living and human, but words, because only with them can one meditate, that is with all possible words, because thinking well requires numerous words. Multiple journey of the thinker who does not have to be contented with canonical knowledge or with the correct proof, but who must throw himself also into myths, stories, and literatures.

Let us call cant the language that uses few words: frozen pond lost in a forest. What can one who writes in such a closed register think of language? Fenced in by a rare idiom, he can speak of atoms, for example, of sailing, of music or of love, but of language! Now I fear that the so-called philosophers of language in fact use only very few words. Is what is lost in breadth gained in finesse or rigor?

Do not say, do, even when you say. Meaning is gained in walking. Enough speech, acts, in speech itself. Too much criticism: works! What's called theory always offers maximum facility with minimal vocabulary. Patient work, that of the writer who navigates the long course of his entire language and who, fearing no waters, writes his language, describes it up to its furthest shores, and tries to exhaust its capacities. Most often language, except for a small part, dozes, just as our neurons sleep. Alas, the tools or the witnesses of intelligence remain lulled to sleep in potentia, waiting for the one who chooses as a career the task of waking them up, of defining his language right up to the fault line, of reviving it whole and proper, of making it think or exist by placing it in a false equilibrium; he combines, tries out long chains of synonyms, all complex and ill at ease, converging at the height of this effort toward a lost nuance. There, he finds what his language does not include. Here he is finally naive. Driven to look, to touch, hear, or taste, obliged to wisdom and sagacity.

Do people know, using the most simply trivial example, that Homo sapiens, at least the French language species, do not use adjectives to signify smells, whereas *sapiens* first of all means to feel or suffer flavors and fragrances? Blue and not color of sky, yellow and not nuance of honey, that is how it is for sight, very well provided for,[5] why then odor of rose or taste of pear? Cruel poverty of

5. Serres uses the word *pourvue*, which contains the word *vue*, sight.—TRANS.

epithet! Even Condillac's statue does not point out this lack, a statue that seems to begin, precisely, with smell, without ever leaving words.

Here then is style: the singular vibration on the confines of language, where a lost variety of green, viewed, demands a new word from the old dictionary, which only gives the thirty neighboring nuances, a vibration of feeling and of the poorly said, an extreme place where like a veil language shivers in the wind, at the edge. Nothing resembles a new thought more than this trembling, at the melted soldering, at the broken clasp, at the fault line of language.

Thus, on a day of a syzygy, Bougainville sails into the unnamed channel where the killer whales and the ju'bartes, packed tight in front of his boom, keep him from arriving.[6]

Plunging as soon as possible into the singular givens of the world, forgeting a language barely learned, never makes one attain naïveté, but restores trite sentences, a false fountain of youth from which one emerges senile; it is better to run through language, as a new end of the world might rise up at the corner of the portolan. The new naif of this event is beginning to grow old.

Touch, hear, taste, breathe, and feel, see, do not speak of the five senses until the end of probative journeys in sciences and narratives. Later, much later. After having turned the last page of every encyclopedia and corpus. Yes, metaphysics and philosophy come after physics and poetics. Having passed through there, his head has become white with knowledge, he has used his tongue with a thousand words. Wily old traveler in sight of virgin islands, he has paid the heavy price of naïveté.

He can instruct because he has the white soul of children. Old, the true naïf instructs the false naïf, who is young. Here, again, the educative couple: two naïvetés that are not twins, the old, authentic, acquired, sapient, true—youthful—and the young, false, crazy, fresh, joyous, indigenous—decrepit. Look for the third.

To work.

6. *Ju'barte* was a name given in the seventeenth and eighteenth centuries to species of rorqual, fin-whale, or finner, especially that found near the coast of New England.—TRANS.

The Stylist and the Grammarian

Why would the philosopher not write? In the name of what must he reduce his meditation to elements of grammar? By what right does one refuse him the right to style?

Seemingly far apart, style and grammar both explore language, with different means. This couple visits the world, knowledge and subjects, God sometimes, starting from language, through methods that you might wish were complementary, that you are surprised to see opposed, since one would not exist without the other, grammar without material, style without rules. Grammar describes, analyzes, seeks to found, sometimes legislates; style experiments, essays. Grammar likes to think it is theoretical and usage experimental. Should philosophy, then, reserve grammar for itself and reject style?

We know this distance that separates or has separated the academic tradition (born in European universities in the Middle Ages, on Greek foundations laid down by a certain Plato and the school of Aristotle, conserved by the Latin Fathers, a tradition that has lasted without notable interruption until today in all Western countries, France included) from another line—less stable, rarer, not very professionalized because linked to certain inimitable individual talents, and having no school or disciples because inimitable— a line that doubtless appeared in France, from Montaigne up to the eighteenth century, but also in Germany, from Goethe to Nietzsche. The grandeur of Plato and the site that he occupies, at the origin of the bifurcation, result from the fact that in his work he united grammatical debate and stylistic exploration, that he wrote *The Theaetetus* and *The Symposium*.

These two halves of philosophy, going along on opposite sides, have little desire to reunite and, far from loving each other, are rivals and heap anathemas and sarcasms on each other. Nevertheless, in certain works, they desire each other and meet, hermaphrodites, not understanding, at the moment of fusion, why mathematical analysis would expel refined language, why the writer, never attaining by right the title of philosopher, ridicules from time to time Honorius, Marphurius, and Janotus of Bragmardo—those risible reasoners.

Can one, peacefully, conceive that a similar division could become complementary? The mathematician will know the world better and even his own language if he consents to physics, the physicist will know things better and even his own tools if he comes round to technology, the technician if he learns craft, and the craftsman if he attains to the work of art. The grammarian-philosopher will know language, knowledge, and the world better if he tolerates style and opens himself to its exploits. Conversely, you can imagine the progress of the artist when he turns to craft, that of the craftsman when he turns himself into a technician, that of the technician . . . and so on until the end of the road, toward mathematics and logic. A double route for the philosopher. And thus, complementarily, the stylist cannot even write without a prior obedience to grammar, without logic or rules of meaning, syntax or semantics. If he truly writes, he indeed consents to this.

But he does not make the rules or the laws explicit. The grammarian, for his part, never deploys the language of which he nonetheless speaks subtly and accurately. One presupposes the other: use, deployment imply the rule that implies a whole philosophy; but grammar presupposes a language that could not have existed without its odysseys. Fact precedes law, but law precedes fact. The work anticipates its logic in the time of history, and philosophy arises when evening comes, but the rules anticipate their application in the ideal and logical time of knowledge and the philosopher awakens at dawn.

Now if the stylist rarely needs grammar and can transgress it in his refined gesture of invention, if the grammarian never gives himself over to style among his delicate minutiae of analysis, it is nonetheless true that the philosopher, present on both fronts, needs to know the gesture of both, and must become, if possible, one and the other. Noon. In the name of what ablative principle would he reduce himself to the theory of elements, given that the positive work of language consists also of accompanying him to his outermost borders and toward his future?

The grammarian-analyst willingly banishes myth, poetry, or literature because of their confused or obscure or, at the very least, shrouded contents, because he seeks the clear and distinct, the explicit, and solicits debate between distinct positions. To his mind, narrative never knows what it is saying.

The stylist laughs at the grammarian, Rabelais at Janotus,

Molière at Marphuris, Marivaux at Honorius, and Musset at Blazius; literature makes fun of the academy, or the academy laughs at university professors for their lowly hatreds that spread terror in times of implacable war, one-fourth of a badly split hair, but laughs, especially, at their immobility. The analyst clarifies, but does not move, indefinitely interpreting, arguing without a break. Does the philosophical grammar of our time go further than it did in the eighteenth century, does that of the eighteenth century go beyond medieval theories, did these surpass antiquity? No. In these fascinating places, philosophy discovers something like a limit point, from which it relentlessly derives debate as one draws water from a well, no more able to walk than Zeno, motionless in his giant stride. It illuminates, certainly, but it never moves. Certainly, it clarifies, but at the cost of a technical language that is restrained, pointed, closed, that often turns into algorithm, quickly inaccessible to whoever does not speak it, as was formerly the case with scholasticism, as if school complacently drives away those who do not have the means to participate in the conversation. Does philosophical grammar clarify as well, at the cost of the thickest obscurity?

As if the obscure balanced itself out, as if the implied remained accessible to everyone. As if language were taking revenge in both cases. You must always pay in the currency you want to earn. Do you wish to analyze? You will not cease to do so, without ever leaving the same point, as if you had gotten hold of an infinite well from which dichotomy gives birth to itself. Do you seek to clarify? You will not cease to bring light until the fires are extinguished. Do you want to interpret? Do not stop: implication returns inexhaustibly. Do you want to debate? Debating begets itself because war gives birth only to war, passing over the belly of problems and of the dead, stomping on the same place. In the same way, rigorous philosophies of communication become incommunicable because of their technical nature.

The efforts or works of the grammarian and of the stylist are as similar as they are opposed to one another. Given over to enshrouding as if to vertigo, they develop the obscure; one through comprehension, justness or accuracy, and depth, the other through expansion, breadth, and movement. These exhibited interpretations come at a high price: in both cases one must pay, whereas each thinks he is not paying. But you pay for every-thing: even progress, even democratic liberties, even atheism, and sometimes dearly. On top of that, the spending granted must be regulated by the currency that circulates in the market where one does one's business: in coin in the commercial district, in tender-ness in the exchange of love, in signatures for legal contracts, else-where sometimes with blood and life. If one must always spend or pay to know, one must consequently settle one's debt, there, in knowledge currency. Clarity is paid for in narrowness, and lofty views by imprecision. Clarification is paid for with statistics and sterility, invention and speed with confusion and obscurity. Even in philosophy, no one has ever succeeded in having his cake and eating it too. To each his risk. The one accepts that his feet will get caught in his shoelaces, the other that he will only lightly touch the ground. Walking, running use up a bit of enlightment; analy-sis leaves fecundity behind. A question of scale: what do micro-scope and telescope, detail and screen squander and gain? In the same way, liberty is exchanged for constraints and progress is paid for with certain regressions. One must look at the balance sheet, that's all.

Each one counts the other's loss in order to say to him amicably: I understand nothing of what you are saying. The grammarian to the stylist, Get out of here, confused and irrational mind. The styl-ist, You are always right in what you advance and claim, I admit it. So? Wily, prudent, rigorous, circumspect, you advance one-half a millimeter per century. During this time, inattentive, courageous, intuitive, I create meaning, Yes, meaning about life, the world, the tragic, knowledge even, love, neighborly relations, and the swal-lows who bear spring on their wings. I make language live at the price of clarity. You clarify language at the cost of its life. If, in order to run, I analyzed the movement of bones, muscles, and neurons, my intentions and goals, reasons and proportions, I would never leave the starting block. The grammarian says: You know nothing. You do nothing, responds the stylist.

Both are correct. The philosopher knows but he also does, work-ing at both jobs on a medium scale.

The analyst cuts up, makes distinctions in order to recognize the elements, of language, for example. But dichotomy or separation do not have a monopoly on the search for the elementary. Other operations remain possible, in all sciences or research, and for example in chemistry: the weight, the mixture of one body with another or the contact of both, the reactions, the examination or the control of variations in a function or process respect ties and connections destroyed by division and allow the presence of a metal to be recognized, the authenticity of an alloy, its genuine worth, in other words, the truth of the analysis. Necessary methods if analysis fails, welcome even if it turns out to be aggressive, because cutting up the links does not leave things as they were. The same is true of philosophy and of language: the philosopher-writer *tries things out, he essays.*

He experiences, experiments. He tests, he assays: two ancient verbs of ancient chemistry, of alchemy even, that have returned to common usage. French still uses the word *têt* (test) in laboratories—an ancient beaker or resistant earthen pot used for assays or for testing gold, but no longer speaks of assay in terms of weighing.

The philosopher-writer experiments on language by constructing it, just as the gesture of the artisan continues, prolongs the lineage of his art, musical staff or line of meaning, and as much as it can, advances. The analyst stops, breaks, theorizes: the writer pursues, maintains connections, fabricates, because he believes that one knows nothing of what one has not practiced professionally. Cant produces a sterile knowledge of dead things. To know language one must make it, too. One must test or assay it.

A faithful assay or essay sometimes, often, produces a negative, opposed, nonsensical result. Objects take revenge just as language does, just as the earth does once one no longer works it. They reserve the unexpected, do not react as foreseen. Experimentation carries a risk—of the aleatory, the unknown.

One exposes oneself when one makes, one imposes oneself when one unmakes. When one unmakes, one is never wrong, in effect. I know of no better way to be always right. I do not believe I know, on the other hand, a better definition of man than the old adage *errare humanum est,* to which I say, Whoever makes mistakes is human. At least he tried.

Fragile, naked, precariously balanced, the writer relies only on talent that never has the solidity of method: with no school to protect him by means of dialogue and a fixed position in the group, without imitator or master, he explores alone. He can thus miss, make mistakes, or lose himself. He bears this possible error and this potential fall like wounds to the flank of his work. The pain and courage of wandering in order to pay for newness. Because, each morning, strange, unpredictable paths present themselves that are so attractive and beautiful that he gets up in haste, at dawn, enthusiastic about landscapes to be crossed, pressed to take up the voyage again in a rarely familiar, often extraordinary world. He never knows who will enter on the next page. Never mind the fall, he tests! If he loses he will not have done anyone wrong, and if he wins he will rejoice. To hell with mistakes, he essays.

Would you have the audacity to speak of the world if you had never traversed it? Just as things differ immensely from what speeches, books, newspapers, magazines, representations say, language has nothing to do with what is said of it when it is not practiced fully.

It is easy to believe that there is no difference between a discourse on Margaux and Margaux, as long as you haven't essayed. Eat and drink. Taste. Test. You believe that a good atlas of the desert takes the place of life with the Tuareg in the Sahara. Leave, go. That a match is reduced to what the newspaper says about it. Take off your clothes, go down on the field, play. Criticism is easy, art difficult. No, love is never proven by words or by love letters. Enough said, let's have acts. History recounted never equals history made, though it brings more glory and money with infinitely less fatigue—that's how strategies are judged in practice. In any case, try.

If not, you lie. You will lie, even if you tell the truth, supposing that you content yourself with talking. Live, taste, leave, do, play, don't copy. The true lie comes from recoiling from the attempt. One willingly believes that the language analyzed by grammar and philosophy equals the live language invented by literature. No. The grammarian, the professor, the philosopher do not write enough to know. Have you noticed, in classrooms, in schools and lecture halls, the absence of true exercise? The examiner or the judge never requires a poem, novella, novel, or a comedy, never a meditation, but always criticism or history, a copy of copies? Why? Because he would not know how to write an answer key. On the contrary, he requires history, criticism, analysis. Why? Because he can and knows how to copy. Why? Because it's easier. Making explores, unmaking undoes. Do not lie, write. The whole truth, but nothing but the truth.

Watch out: it's lethal.

Socrates, an analyst, demands short speeches. He interrupts rhetoricians and rhapsodes, he barks, makes fun of them and torpedoes them. His questions cut up the exposé into brief phrases of dialogue, and his dichotomy brings the proposition back to the minimal length, that of a word.

Why did you just write "demand," in what sense, what kind of demand are you talking about? What speech, why a speech, long, short, what dialogue, why a dialogue, what will you lose by cutting everything? Anyone can let fall on Socrates the blows with which he strikes Protagoras or someone else. With what right do you impose, here and now, this type of argumentation? Under what condition? What do you want? Against whom are you fighting? The length of the preliminaries and the requisite conditions, before the beast in question appears, measure the weight of meanness. Socrates, how you love petty quarreling and victory: Could your soul be so base? Who named you the state's attorney, the implacable prosecutor of humanity? Why do you take the place of those who condemn us and who, someday, will judge you? What resentment pushes you to the perpetual accusation of everyone you meet? By what right this right that you give yourself of pursuing and denouncing? A third Socrates, if you will, can be born, in turn, of such questions posed by Socrates to Socrates, and so on as much as one desires. Here the indefinite well of debate is opened.

Armed with a short sword, the foot soldier advances toward the cavalryman to seek hand-to-hand combat, body to body, his favorite kind. Encumbered by his mount, his caparison, and his chlamys, the Sophist writer falls to the ground, thrown from the saddle, he who is used to galloping on horseback and not to fighting hand to hand, armed with a bow whose arrow flies or with a javelin that he throws. Here he is flat on the ground, fragile, stuck in the earth, Socrates crushes him. With what hatred and by what right?

One breaks up the text with a little fencing rattle that cavilingly details the large network of meanings intersected by the other, and on which faraway, subtle attractions play, from the exordium to the finale and vice versa.

The myrmidon with the small sabre, protected by heavy armor, a chitinous insect, confronts in the closed amphitheater, the retiarius, soft, naked, in mobile netting, a flighty bird. Singular combat of the static and solid foot soldier against the agile and enveloping light infantryman: formerly, the Romans appreciated these two gladiators—reduced models of the cavalry with its lightning movements and of the infantry, stubbornly resistant, rooted in the ground—who are opposed in the collective battle, on the front line, and in the open field.

The sword tears, makes holes, cuts the network, cuts stitch by stitch into the fault lines of false meaning. The retiarius makes the net undulate, an expanse that becomes a hoop net, plane and sphere, wall and prison, gauche surface and mobile volume: in zero dimension, a point or a rolled ball in the gladiator's fist; in one dimension, a long chain of reason unfolded on his shoulder; in two dimensions, cape manuevers displayed before the myrmidon, like a lure that a bull looks at; in three dimensions, an omnipresence, surrounding the body, crossed bonds that attach, seize, suffocate the myrmidion, put him to death.

Does language—analyzed, unravelled by a sabre, phrase by phrase, letter by letter, word by word—maintain the same scope, a similar function as when undulating, mobile, connected, linked, changing unceasingly in appearance, flowing with its local composition, always global even dense as a stone in the hand? Would it not have, in both cases, a polemical or warlike status?

Socrates the footsoldier unseats the cavalryman, Socrates the myrmidon tears the net of the retiarius, Socrates the prop forward or hooker,[7] immobile, his bull neck jutting forward, in the black tunnel of the scrum, toes rooted in the mud up to the ankles, resists every push, tackles to the point of winding the third or three-quarter line who strike the whole heavy mechanism with an imperceptible change in speed. The forward fights foot to foot, the stand-off half, changing feet, reorients the whole fabric of the game from the closed side toward the open side, with a slight or invisible distancing from equilibrium, the fullbacks unceasingly fool each other by catching each other off balance.

7. The hooker gets the ball once it has cleared the legs of his teammates in the scrum.—TRANS.

By the time the analyst distinguishes the right from the left, the third excluded, the stylist has already alighted in the dust, caressing the earth, with a third, dove's foot that, unnoticed, makes the retiarius's net fly toward the bleachers, whereas those in the boxes expected it. Short combat or long: a change of scale. A prop forward advances step by step, meter after meter of earth dearly conquered, a twist of the lower back, a feint or sneak move from behind; one kick in the goal area and the action will shift to sixty meters away. Over what void are you bent here, analyst—the question has rebounded so far away on the long geodesics of language . . . Raise your head above the scrum, see high and long.

The myopic bull, neck lowered on the ochre sand, throws his tons and his horns, in a rectilinear orbit, at the torero in his bright and funereal outfit, pirouetting behind red mariposas and manoletinas, buttocks high, fine, fragile, trembling, the groin and the arch of the thigh exposed, the wrist sensititive to the slightest solicitation. Till when, in what direction the inclination—to the millimeter, to the very half-second? Which of the two, four-footed infantryman or swift-footed runner, will die, in celebrating a decisive moment in the history of the human beast, which of the two, the hoof or its opposite, will kill, in this commemoration of the instant where the collective turned, without knowing or deciding on it, from human to animal sacrifice?

Bull Socrates, globular eyes, bald forehead, fawn's muffle, ugly to the point of being scary, unseats with one blow of his head the disarticulated Sophist puppet. What instant does he commemorate with this hateful parricide? What forgotten moments will we commemorate when the prop forward tackles the three-quarter, when the retiarius strangled the vanquished myrmidon on the bare ground, when the foot soldier unseated the cavalryman, when the analyst convicts the philosopher-writer of nonsense? Whether we go from murder to entertainment, from war to gymnastics, from ritual to language, from spilled blood to philosophy, behavior as well as passions remain constant.

Good trainers say it is impossible to mistake what distinguishes gymnasts' bodies from athletic natures. The latter run, jump, play, whereas the former fight or balance themselves on the beam, as master sailors used to. No athlete is at ease on the trapeze or on the bars, few gymnasts come down to the track or the field. Short, with stocky musculature, with powerful arms and a scapular waist, or else wiry, with powerful upper thighs, spirited. Military recruiting had the benefit, I suppose, of both of these populations. Drafted, Socrates checks in with the gymnasts.

The teacher, a good trainer of intelligences, is never mistaken either, in regard to the same difference in the domain of knowledge. He observes both parallel populations: opinionated workers, with a stubborn will, a narrow horizon and few ideas, efficient and stable, winners, tirelessly returning to the same subject, fixed and obsessive—hedgehogs; rapid intuitors with a subtle sense of smell, numerous fleeting ideas, burgeoning innovators deprived of mastery over their own fecundity, inefficient, unstable, in love with beauty—foxes. Realistic entrepeneurs and miserable aristocrats. The burrowing insect and the migrating bird, the grammarian and the stylist. Don Quixote and Sancho Panza. Today, Panza makes his fortune in science; in ordinary literature, Quixote drags his misery.

Socrates and Plato. No philosophy without this peaceable couple, without this united pair that never existed. Always dueling, finally. Plato—but where had he run off to, afraid, at the moment of the death of his master, the great character missing from *The Phaedo?*—Plato, in the end, writes, once the trial is over, on the cadaver of Socrates, rigid and cold, subtle analyses of the soul: Plato drugs Socrates with hemlock in order to be able to write long and beautifully, plunges the torpedo himself into torpor, gives him a narcotic in order not to find himself torpedoed, immobilized, forever bound to the exhausting dichotomy as infinite in its genre as the most watered-down speech. What wonderful good fortune to keep grammar at a distance without the barking of the grammarian, to follow the law after the death of the legislator, but how tragically sad to commemorate always the same battle for the same execution.

When he writes, the bull is dead. But he never wrote why Socrates was never able to write: exhausted by analysis.

An old savage philosophy where peace cannot intervene except between a derisory Socrates seated on his ass and a beautiful, discomfited Plato perched on his mare, running after pure ideas—Don Quixote and Sancho Panza.

Let writing give grammar its demon and light irony, the height of its views, the breadth of its field; let analysis give style a faultless solidity, and philosophy will be reborn. To ensure a footing in the neighborhood at hand but to predict from afar: no one directs his steps on the mountain, his horse on the road, manages his body, generally, his life, his soul, his family, his budget or drives his car, his thought by doing without this simple and necessary precept, which reunites in one glance the local and the global, the universal and the singular, but whose disjunction produces a single laughable idiocy, fall, or immobility; Quixote in windmills and discomfiture, Sancho cultivating banality.

No philosophy without this appeased pair, laughing about useless battles that have simply become rituals, through commemoration. But now that we truly remember the cadavers that lie between us, that of the sacrificed cock on top of that of the condemned Socrates, of the bull or the matador, of the retiarius and the myrmidon, of the foot soldier and the cavalryman, now that we remember this original sin of linguistic disputes, the archaic execution, what good is the ritual of commemoration? What good does it do to make the stylist and the grammarian fight in the arena of language?

If philosophy, friend of wisdom, or, more grammatically, thus with more stylistic elegance, *learned in love,* has as a goal what it claims to have in its name, tomorrow it will speak, all at once, of language, and will ask for its support, more than for the support of analysis and rhetoric together, for that of myths and religions, technologies and sciences—third included.

That day the adventure will begin again.

A youthful memory: Leibniz completes his *Discours sur la conformité de la foi avec la raison* [Discourse on the conformity of faith with reason] with Bayle's funeral. "Now my adversary," Leibniz says, "sees God face to face—and that I am right." Just beforehand, he had cited great predecessors, including Abelard, who suffered in their flesh as payment for their discussions. Leibniz wins because Bayle is dead. The tribunal passes sentence, condemns, and one understands the weight of the punishment, finally: Dantesque. *The Divine Comedy* also takes revenge post mortem, in the three supernatural spaces outlined by the sentence. The vengeance of writing and of philosophy, like that of the atomic bomb, overkills.

Not only kills but condemns or still saves after death. In the sciences, theories change, not through the marvelous power of their veracity, but because the holders of adverse theories retire, and therefore are dead to the colloquia and to the administration; and there is always some historian to unearth the cadavers and condemn once again some forgotten inventor to wander without rest in the hell of error and deceptive shadows. History: a well of resentments.

Here, again, the stake of discourse—the conformity of reason and faith—is settled by death. Because if argumentative and pugnacious reason drives the adversary to death, faith, in and of itself, reveals to us what comes after death. Thus conformity—I mean the thing and the cause that faith and reason have in common—is again death. Speculatively, certainly, but also practically, in the written discussion between Leibniz and Bayle, up to the splendid funeral of the latter who is immolated at the entrance to the tribunal of the *Theodicy*. Behind the tribunal, where God himself appears, accused, appears the one where the philosopher, a writer, triumphs.

Thus Leibniz constructs the courtroom, and there he pleads the divine cause. He places his feet—he establishes himself—on Bayle's tomb; he, the saintly and reasonable philosopher, who will resolve the question and obtain the proper sentence. In the same way, Plato stands on the funeral and the tomb of Socrates. Does this position bring all philosophers close together? Does philosophical reason always need a murder to establish itself?

Recently an important change occurred: my feet have not rested on the—full—tomb of any particular body, but on the—empty—cenotaph of humankind in its entirety, ever since "Thanatocracy," *Statues*, and *The Natural Contract*.[8] Today, at the tribunal of reason and of science, the philosopher pleads for the survival of men on Earth, pleads that the abominable black box may long remain empty.

No more individual executions, but rather the demands of specific lives: we no longer fight against anyone but ourselves. None of us are opposed to the other, rather we all live as thirds.

A certain history is being completed. Is a new one beginning?

---

8. Cf. "Trahison: La Thanatocratie"[Treason: Thanatocracy], in *Hermès III, La Traduction* (Paris: Minuit, 1974), pp. 73–104.—TRANS.

Peace over the Species

A highway encircles Stanford University; inside this belt, fifteen thousand women and men write, read, experiment, print, calculate, frequently get together to talk, and sometimes to think, devoted to language and to codes. Past the confines of the campus, three gently rolling hills, most often bare, sometimes green, provide a refuge for hikers who if they are silent and walk quietly can find blue jays and kestrel falcons, rare rattlesnakes and many harmless serpents, a kite and an enormous tarantula, in addition to the troop of heifers, the tacit counterpart to the students and researchers below.

There one sees only the sun or the moon, the bay in the distance, the San Andreas Fault close by, and hears nothing but the wind, the canonical chirping of a bird so easy to imitate that the singer soon obligingly responds, one communicates there through means other than language: would this be one of the sites of another kind of knowledge?

Refusing to transport, with a walkman, the language of one into the silence of the other, the solitary person would, instead, attempt to bring the latter, the ancient, into the new one; a disciple of Saint Francis, he speaks to the birds, but above all he listens.

This then is what animals do not speak about.

Weddings of the Earth with Its Successive Masters

Latecomers, still astonishing the Earth with their youth, gauche, rigid, stiff, only a few million years old, therefore maladapted, arrogant about their little science, hominids believe themselves to be first, because they arrive last. Inanimate matter, flora and fauna are often older than they. Hominids seem not to know that their history, new and recent, repeats a thousand already completed cycles.

As soon as each of the living species appeared in the light, the others saw it actively try to conquer the whole Earth, flora and fauna, in their totality, present and past, space, time, energy, all the food, from the sun to the entrails of the globe.

Plants, fish, reptiles, birds, insects, mammals, each in turn and time after time, in successive waves, wrenched mastery and empire from life, each according to his means and his strategy, size, power, force, number, ruse, and meanness, to the very limit of power and glory.

And all without exception, from the worm to the bull, from the fern to the sequoia, from the mosquito to the cow, from the serpent to the whale, era by era, became kings: the wolf, the rat, the ocelot, the wapiti . . . Approaching them, we still recognize today, on their garments or their body, in their carriage or the length of their stride, the majesty of their reign and their ancient dignity. Here they are at the summit.

At this point, it was necessary, all of a sudden, to decide. Each specialized species, having reached the extreme limits of appropriation, pulled the inanimate world, in all its generality, down its narrow slope. The new master invades the whole of the Earth: the surface of the globe suddenly finds itself crawling with millions of lizards . . . nothing new under the sun; rational reproduction covers the manifold and burgeoning real; or rather, depending on whoever seizes the upper hand, in the sole and generalized termitarium, the termite has nothing to eat except an identical termite.

Having arrived at its culmination, this species eliminates all the others and destroys the Earth, unbalanced and in danger of dying from this simplification; in turn, the Earth places the queen species in danger of extinction from the species' excessive triumph. Indeed, when only rats exist, how will the rats be able to continue to exist among rats alone?

On this vertiginous threshold, one by one, in the course of time and of millions of millennia, each species presented itself in turn: and the Earth judged them.

Here and there, in the universe, other earths, maybe, disappeared as a result of this challenge, of their final battle against the temporary master, but the constant and hyperarchaic presence of our Earth, here below, shows that at this temporal threshold, endlessly repeated throughout our evolution, Mother Earth always got the last word.

Each reign recoiled before the Mother.

Species disappeared, and others, literally, were humbled. Those that survived remained because they renounced unique mastery, power and glory, the horrifying competition, when they were faced with the announcement of collective death that would immediately follow definitive victory. In order to survive, then, in themselves and by themselves, they made this mute decision, tacitly imprinted in their coded gene. There lies the mark of their humility.

Yes, they humbled themselves before the Earth, abandoned the pinnacle and entered her: obedient to her constraints, they dove to melt in the depths of the seas or slid beneath her surface without disturbing it by slipping into the heavy swell, drilled black trenches into the humus or the rocks, disappeared in the turbulences of high-altitude regions or linked themselves together, immobile, in an inextricable network of creepers and branches to form a mass of rain forests or equatorial forests . . . all, in the end, dissolved, mixed, melted into nature, thus named because it gave back birth, silently, communitarily, to those who had just abandoned forever the arrogance of their ancient destiny, the paranoid project of occupying the whole Earth for themselves alone; abandoning their haughty strategy to reunite with the enslaved obedience of instinct, the faultless harmonic fold of Mother Earth, who, then, would safeguard them.

Today, the animal seems to bend, humbled, before man. Our forgetting induces this stupid illusion. Obedience reflects, in all places and times, the image of command.

Too young, having arrived late, only a few million years old, we never acquired the memory of previous reigns: the era of the creeper, that of the spider, of the scarab, the reign of the mammoth, of the fly, or of the cow. But language remembers: because the name that *homo* was given comes to him from humility.

Proud, arrogant, filled with power and glory or actively stretched toward them, *homo humilis* seems not to know that his destiny, written in his name (just as the primordial, final, and definitive decision of plants and animals is mutely inscribed in the genome of the species) will one day lead him to humble himself. To dissolve, to mix, to hide in the humus, our first parent, when faced with the risk of death and burial. Too fond of taking command, we will all bow, in our turn, before this Earth that bears the same name we do.

Contrary to our illusions, if animals humble themselves, heads bent to the earth and eyes lowered, they thereby show us, time after time, that they once played, each in turn, the role of men.

Humbled, all the living were once called men. Were men. Kings, they enjoyed the summit, threw down the virile challenge of mastery before their definitive retreat. Our language retells this, the look of the sea lion expresses it, it can be counted in the stripes of the tiger's dress, read in the ruddy hourglass of the black widow or deciphered in the calm braids of the anaconda.

All humans, before their dissolution into humus and instinct, conserve behind them their true original sin, forever stable in their genome: to have been men, thus kings, new, glorious, powerful, and so madly competitive that they forgot the Earth. Obedient now from having commanded so much, they have abandoned this intelligence in favor of bestiality. Savage and sage.

This sin, everyone keeps it, fixedly, behind them, and their whole instinctive existence continues to arrange itself in memory—but we hold it before us, like our collective project. Not at all original: terminal. Next, final—but not primitive.

Here we are in turn, the last, at the pinnacle of power, at the very instant of committing the sin. Will we leave paradise?

I have to say to my grandchildren that I still remember a childhood in a calm countryside that provided plenty of delicious fruit.

Choose: empire or Earth? Up to now the latter has won.

I seek a middle path between royal, arrogant, imbecile intelligence and harmonious, polished, humble instinct, obedient with dumb platitudinousness for having commanded maldly.

Thus I never leave the—third—path on the crest between the institutions of science and the hills of silence.

Peace and Life through Invention. Troubadour.
Learning, forgetting. With the exception of very rare cases—less than ten assuredly for four millennia of known history, those who almost always sign their names to mathematical and musical works (two languages with a thousand values because they are deprived of discursive meaning)—one encounters no natural, immediate and savage genius. Those who wait for inspiration will never produce anything but wind, both of which are aerophagic. Everything always comes from work, including the free gift of the idea that arrives. To give oneself over, here and now, in one go, to no matter what, without preparation, ends in *art brut* whose interest is

confined to pyschopathology or to fashion: an ephemeral bubble worthy of the stage and of buffoons.

Artwork, let's look at the word. The work has a worker as its author, a craftsman by training, who has become expert in his particular material: forms, colors, images, for those kinds of craftsmen, language for me, marble or landscape for others. Before claiming to produce new thoughts, one must, for example, hear the vowels: a worker, a craftsman of writing distributes them in a sentence and on the page like a painter his reds among his greens, or a composer the brass instruments overlaying the percussion section, never just any old way. Such is the case for consonants or subordinate clauses: a lengthy labor on a sheet as full of holes as the barrel of Danaid, a Sisyphean task so undefined that one spends one's life at it. To create: to give oneself over to nothing but that, from dawn till the throes of death.

All of this presupposes the best health: devouring the body with its flame, creation exhausts to death and kills in the flower of youth whoever does not resist with force: Raphael, Mozart, Schubert, around thirty, Balzac and St. Thomas Aquinas, around forty. Before beginning to rhyme, the elder Corneille would get undressed to roll himself up, completely naked, in homespun blankets in which he would sweat abundantly, as in a sauna: the work of genius transpires from the body like a secretion. It emerges from the glands. Rousseau and Diderot walked dozens of kilometers, every day. New ideas come from athletes. In Greek the nickname *Plato* signifies broad-shouldered. One must imagine the great philosophers as rugby players. In rigging three masts en route from Saint Malo to Baltimore, Chateaubriand outclassed the sailors in gymnastics and acrobatics.

Malebranche was asked how and why He had created the world, with its procession of suffering and trials, of crimes and abominations, this infinite God who could so easily have rested, eternally enjoying his intelligence and renewed happinesses; the philosopher would customarily reply that no one creates except through an excess of strength: thus the universe is born from the excess strength of its maker. In practice, nothing is more true. With greater strength, the work comes; from weakness, nothing.

One thus meets few sick, drugged, weak, or melancholic geniuses. Doubting, yes: pathological, no. The romantic and deceptive publicity in favor of the mad, the unhinged, or the unbalanced, whose work runs on neurosis or chemicals, has produced many sterile emulations: nothing comes out of an injection or a whiskey flask. Or, rather: supposing the worker starts out weak and languishing, the work, small and growing, quickly functions, for him, as a support, and unceasingly reinforces the worker. The work inhabits force, then power lodges in the work; one feeds off the other which nourishes itself with it, so that both, in a spiraling symbiosis, grow from each other by increasing their resistance to the attraction of death.

What is called the immortality of chefs d'oeuvre simply results from this positive volute that is nourished and expands by returning to itself, like a whirlpool or a galaxy. Vital health produces of itself, then the product rebounds on life, until it conquers morbidity as well as mortality. Thus what was born two thousand years ago still lives intensely. If the work needs the worker, at a certain point the latter needs only the work: it's up to the worker to give his body and his life, the work gives it back with interest. Whence, in the end, victory over death.

Thus there exists a hygienics, yes, a diet of the work. High-level sportsmen live like monks, and creators live like these athletes. Do you seek to invent or to produce? Begin with exercise, seven regular hours of sleep, and a strict diet. The hardest life and the most demanding discipline: asceticism and austerity. Resist fiercely the talk around you that claims the opposite. All that debilitates sterilizes: alcohol, smoking, late nights, and pharmaceuticals. Do not resist only narcotics, but especially social chemistry, by far the strongest and thus the worst: the media, conventional fashions. Everyone always says the same thing and, like the flow of influence, descends the steepest slope together.

The work of art erects a dam against this erosion. A victory over death, it identifies with life, and there is no known life except an individual one. Singular. Original. Solitary. Stubborn. The work makes up an animal species unto itself, since its tree, phylogenetic, produces individual fruits or buds, books, music, films, or poems. It comes, then, from a unique disposition of neurons and blood vessels. Never from collective banality. The opposite of fashion, opposed to what is said, it resists the media—that is, the middling—by definition.

The goal of instruction is the end of instruction, that is to say invention. Invention is the only true intellectual act, the only act of intelligence. The rest? Copying, cheating, reproduction, laziness, convention, battle, sleep. Only discovery awakens. Only invention proves that one truly thinks what one thinks, whatever that may be. I think therefore I invent, I invent therefore I think: the only proof that a scientist works or that a writer writes. Why work, why write otherwise? In all other cases, they sleep or fight and prepare to die badly. They repeat. The inventive breath alone gives life, because life invents. The absence of invention proves, by counterexample, the absence of the work and of thought. The one who does not invent works somewhere other than in intelligence. Brutish. Somewhere other than life. Dead.

The institutions of culture, of teaching, or of research, those that live on messages, repeated images, or printed copies, the great mammoths that are the universities, media, and publishing, the ideocracies also, surround themselves with a mass of solid artifices that forbid invention or break it, that fear it like the greatest danger. Inventors scare them, just as the saints placed their churches in danger; the cardinals chased the saints from the church because they were troubled by them. The more institutions evolve toward the gigantic, the better the counterconditions are for the exercise of thought. Do you want to create? You are in danger.

Invention, light, laughs at the heavy mammoth; solitary, it knows nothing of the collective great animal; sweet, it avoids the hatred that holds this collective together. All my life I have marveled at the hatred of intelligence that makes up the tacit social contract of so-called intellectual establishments. Invention, agile, rapid, shakes the soft belly of the slow beast; the intent of discovery doubtless carries in itself a subtlety that is unbearable to large organizations, which can only continue to exist if they consume redundancy and forbid freedom of thought.

One calls information a quantity proportional to rarity. Precisely scientific, this definition surprises whoever hears the other kind of information being spread about and disseminated to the point of redundancy. This is the misunderstanding: what is propagated and becomes probable, in making the obedient napes bend, is called entropy; inversely, negentropy grows in proportion to improbability. Information, negentropic and thus not very probable, goes against the irreversible course of entropy, which crumbles toward disorder and nondifferentiation.

This last flow wears away the relief, levels it, dissolves all sorts of rocks and combines them, the river leads toward the sea, mixed with increasingly slow and muddied waters, undifferentiated sand, while the dam, rare, creates difference: it resists the descent that ancient language designated by the verb to gulp down *[avaler]*, to fall downstream *[vers l'aval]*. All known sources are reduced to these dams. In order, then, for invention, as one says, to flow from the source, this resistance must intervene, at some point and somewhere; doubtless, that is enough. Entropy descends, information goes back upstream, the former toward the most probable, the latter toward the rare.

Resist. The current, the fall, dissolution, disorder, time. The sugar cube cannot defend itself against water, which dissolves it but which cannot cut into the diamond. One could easily define work as the complete set of operations that would permit drawing out the sugar, extracting it and crystallizing it, from the water in which it entered into a solution: dissolving it, on the other hand, illustrates the opposite of work. In the first case, you need energy, not in the second. As the saying goes, it happens all by itself.

Because the work and the worker belong to the same family as the word *energy*, what is the nature of the work that makes the worker? A bank of energy, a depot of power like a lake upstream from a dam, a mine of coal, a pool of oil, some kind of capital. In all cases: accumulated time. Saturated with information, inexhaustible, the work of art not only resists time as it passes but also reverses it.

It is easy to reckon the temporal difference between the work of art and the luxury object, for example. The latter costs quite a lot when fashion displays it, but a few years later it is difficult to sell and only at a low price; on the other hand, their paintings saved neither Van Gogh from indigence nor Gauguin from black misery, and one hundred parasites now wrench their works from each other for the weight of gold or yen. In the equation where time equals money, one rises and the other falls.

Here a world other than the one in which we live is defined: here, the earth and the stars turn in the opposite direction. Each day Molière gets younger and makes my grandchildren laugh, and the Bastille Opera house, before it is even born, is looking dreadfully old. Resistance is not enough, because there has never been a bridge that on some disastrous day a river did not carry away, or a frightened virgin who did not cede to the advances of a rather hairy fawn. Time does not cease its work of usury, so that, in order to get the better of it, one must swim upstream. Coming from the source, the water makes the low watermark of the dammed lake rise toward the top without going downstream.

You will recognize the work and the authentic worker from this infallible sign: both together make you younger. They will die children, from having had to run toward the origin of the world. To create means to go toward the hands of the divine worker at the dawn of things. To reverse time.

As rarity, information runs, then, in the opposite direction from that of information as dissemination. Or rather: the order that composes crystal, the pentagon of rose windows, the twinned cell from which human offspring is born, reverses the order that makes all obedient napes bend in parallel. As if certain things went up the very stream that the orders men give themselves go down. One requires energy, work, and power, the other falls all by itself. Two worlds, two flows or stellar rotations, two kinds of time: that of the work of art follows life, the other sinks with death and history. We once again encounter the two foci.

Resisting is not enough; because of invariance, the direction, the action of movement must be reversed.

If you seek to create, love springs, fountains, precious stones, the high summits of mountains, the layers of the onion, the leaves of the artichoke, the look of the sea lion, germinal cells, children, all filled to bursting with information like blue supergiants and flee the spendthrifts that waste information: newspapers, what's called news, spreading rumor.

Nevertheless, certain works have met with success: they must certainly have suited the most common taste to gain favor at once. Yes and no, and, in the end, more like no.

To resist the ratings, let's distinguish two types of success. Yes, the first follows fashion: and immediately proves it by transforming itself the next day into a flop. It does not last out the month, sometimes the week; it cannot survive time in general. How many books temporarily in vogue yesterday now burden the remainder tables? In this instance, success does not engender its succession.

Conversely, as if by a miracle, the other kind of success plunges to the very depth of the live works of the moment, intuits them, surveys them, awakens them, liberates them, arouses them. This second triumph lasts. I hope this for all. But do not be mistaken: nothing is more difficult than trying to determine of what our present consists. What everyone says of it, far from clarifying it, masks and conceals it. Do not forget that the media repeat what those who control them today were saying when they were twenty years old: they are at least a generation behind and sometimes two. Thus you must search passionately for what you are and not for what they say you are. Don't listen to anyone. Resist the torrent of influences, the medals.

This is the only means of liberating the present, which is defined precisely by the rare, miraculous, information-saturated meeting of the work with the live, latent forces that condition it, but which only the work can deliver. The contemporary moment is created through the work of art more than the work is fabricated by the contemporary moment. Time, which always sleeps, is awakened by creation, just as God aroused Eve, the dream of whom was gasping for breath beneath Adam's rib. In this case, success assures and begets succession: the succession of time follows the success of the work and not vice versa.

To find the contemporary, a difficult thing. To discover what one is, a much rarer invention still.

It seems to me that one can only create in the straight grain of culture that is incarnated in the flesh of its flesh. I stammer when I express myself in any language other than my own, while my exactitude seeks and finds to say in French something that my body has carried for millennia in my maternal tongue, Occitan, midway between Spanish and Italian, the two other leaves of a clover with a Latin peduncle, but spread in Celtic land, in the West more than the East, thus more English than Mediterranean. That is the image that my coat of arms carries, that tattooing of my skin, the imprinting of my genetic code, half-breed. Does one only invent something new when it issues from the deepest roots? Like a bolt of lightning, the present idea connects the black and forgotten earth with the unbreathable stratosphere of the future. It is thus necessary to declare our specificity.

In the realm of rarity, the demanding French tradition, ironic and fine, learned but light, reserved beneath understatement, haughtiness and secrecy, always keeps way ahead of its rivals or emulators, but this primacy often goes unrecognized, because of its hard nature, or precisely, because of the quantity of information, tucked away beneath reserve. Rome, Florence, or Venice gives itself more readily than Paris, a sublime rather than amiable city, one that is difficult to understand. In the same way, Couperin and Corneille, infinitely arduous, are harder to understand than Beethoven or Shakespeare, who do not hesitate to use any means to gain our favor. We refuse ourselves charm and comforts, so that we pass for unreachable, and sometimes, for arrogant. That modesty seems proud, that is our paradox! Thus, always in danger of leaving success to more rapid and more certain seducers, France runs the fatal risk of keeping itself from the French themselves; its culture is unceasingly threatened with ruin from this excess or this distance. When debility is the fashion, our language, for example, rare, demanding, artistic, loses. Coca-Cola always beats Sauternes, hands down. Flat out. Flat.

In addition, we criticize ourselves to the point of exasperation and exclusion, so that in a century in which advertising never waits for someone else to pay you a compliment, we defeat ourselves in all competitions, which are now global.

It is not only in the fine arts that this improbable haughtiness makes our lives so difficult: we do not like half measures in anything. Our teams play soccer and rugby divinely or (typically) collapse when the rarest of talents is lacking. A culture makes its nature known as much in stadiums as in other places. Ours, the most difficult, demands still more austerity than thousands of others that refuse themselves little in the way of indulgences.

Nothing, then, is more difficult than to create in France, but we are condemned to produce in this difference. Resist imports then, most often corrupted. You will always be bad at knockoffs. Halfbreed, yes; counterfeit, no.

To create, one must know everything and thus have worked prodigiously; this necessary condition no longer suffices. Because the weight of the past or science crushes and sterilizes: no one produces less than a historian, a professor, or worse, a critic. To analyze or to judge, that is proper to the impotent, who, together, enjoy all power.

Thus, with his whole body, all his passion, his anger, and his strained liberty, whoever wants to create resists the power of knowledge, both the works that have already been made and the institutions that feed on them. This signifies, to put it plainly: leave everything that reassures, take the greatest risks. One must instruct oneself as much as a possible, at the beginning, in order to train oneself: everything comes from work; learn and fabricate without respite. I now branch off to maintain the opposite.

Learn everything, certainly, but only in order to know nothing. Doubt in order to create. I thus resist in order to finish with my preceding speech.

I have the urge to tell fortunes, the only adventure still possible in contemporary times, the only game in which the loser takes all and the winner often takes nothing. No, the philosopher who seeks does not employ method, the exodus without a path remains his only sojourn and his blank book. He does not plod along or travel by following a map that would retrace an already explored space; he has chosen to wander. Wandering includes the risk of error and distraction. Where are you going? I don't know. Where are you coming from? I try not to remember. Through where do you pass? Everywhere and through as many places as possible, encyclopedically, but I try to forget. Refuse to recognize your references. There are few supports in the desert. Philosophy lives and is displaced in this austere and desertlike landscape where a whole people wandered for a generation and waited and saw nothing of the promised land. It does not seek a spring, a well, a mountain or a statue, inventions or local discoveries, but a global world, where its nephews can live.

Positive sciences employ methods and results: whoever mathematizes, programs, manipulates phenomena in the laboratory, or launches an opinion poll, almost always knows what he is doing; and, when he doesn't know, he sometimes invents.

Thus, as soon as slanderous tongues claim that I almost never know what I am doing or am going to think when I dedicate myself to philosophy, take them, I beg of you, at their word. If the philosopher follows a method or a school, the philosopher dies in the rigidity of dogma or because what a teacher said has vitrified his thought; if he obtains local results, his discipline happily becomes a science, lost forever to philosophy.

Which I must now define: philosophy devotes itself to anticipating future knowledge and practices on a global scale. A scientist discovers or invents in the lacunae of a method, the failures of experiments, the incompleteness of results or the toppling of a theory, but the philosopher has neither theory nor experiments nor method, thus even less their gaps or their flip sides. The scientist, always recognizable, points to his time; one recognizes the philosopher in terms of whether or not he has brought the future: if he misses it, he does not exist. Philosophy, very rare, exists if and only if it sets aside and carves out a space that history will inhabit, just as the Middle Ages were lodged in a sort of Augustinized Aristotle, the Renaissance in Plato, and modern times in Descartes, Leibniz, and Bacon. The work of a philosopher, if and when it takes place, establishes a ground that will found local inventions to come. It carries generality, the earth or the atmosphere of the history of science itself and the liberty of art, the opening of knowledge and the house of pity. Far from being produced, as it is today, by the divisions of previous knowledge and as one among them, philosophy thus has the function of engendering the next knowledge in its global culture, which is why, today, it dreams of the third instruction.

This invention and the hope of it thus entice one to an adventure from which one does not return and that can be described in terms of exodus and not of method, of birth and crossbreeding, as wandering rather than as an itinerary or a curriculum, and as a desert without reference points rather than as a discipline in the form of a staked-out space—all dangerous and risky terms that can be understood as myths or poems in order to exclude them from thought, when one is traveling along the most certain paths, but which are valuable as elements of an anthropology of discovery or an ethic, or better yet as a simple hygienics, for those who cast themselves into this folly with no hope of recompense. Christopher Columbus invents the West Indies; does not return the way he came; wanders, deprived of an atlas, along an oceanic expanse without reference points; resists the pressure of his peers; his exodus remains unaware that he finally sees a large whole, which will be named after somebody else. What does it matter? He begets a time.

A few centuries ago, classical philosophers strove for *Rules*, in imitation of monasteries, but for governing the mind. Would I dare to rewrite some rules for losing your mind, or for messing up the play of the advertising subject and its lingo, the play of ambition in the city or of dominant systems? Learn everything, first; then, when the time has come, throw everything that you own into the fire, including your shoes, go naked. Only third innocence invents. If you want to lose your soul, work to save it, because he who seems to have lost it is finally the one who saves it. Only the one who has played the riskiest, the most absurd, the most mortal game discovers; the game of always losing ends up winning in another world— that of things themselves.

Men of all cultures have only ever invented, whatever the domain, if they knew they were going to die and because they knew how to live and think close to death, our ultimate limitation and most extreme source. The terrible place whence all life comes.

Creation resists death, by reinventing life: that is called resurrection.

Another Name for the Third-Instructed. Troubadour.
I do not seek, I find—and only write if I find. Nothing in my books, in any place, is revived from elsewhere. What is more lively, at the first break of dawn, than the improbable unexpectedness, so alert to time, of finding?

Who is more profoundly boring than the repetitive reasoner who copies or seems to construct by constantly repositioning the same cube? Ruminating on the past—what a system! Repeating a method—what laziness! Method seeks but does not find.

Yet, reader, what ease in recognizing yourself in a text because you always start the same one again: by beginning again, you believe you understand, whereas, spoiled, you scratch yourself in the same place. On the contrary, who hears the one who finds?

For he demands a lot from himself and from those who study him closely: new in each line, his text is not supported by any reprise. The most difficult art is that of infinite melody, which launches itself and risks itself, wandering on the path that it itself invents and that never returns to itself, whose leap is sustained only by its restlessness, exposed, exploring unceasingly another fragment of the earth, flapping like the edge of a flag in the wind, going forward without profit or help, always at the stage of being born, cheerful, in turmoil, tormented, twisted, torturing, strange to hear, emanating from the body's roots like birds taking flight all around the leaves of a tree, burgeoning, divergent, an open exodus that those trouvères, finders who go nimbly from novelties to finds, suffer and chant.

Born under a secret name, I finally found my ancestors; I have always written like a troubadour.

The Generative Couple of History. Death and Immortality

Despite its glorious name, the power that one accords it and its theatrical gesture, creation cannot survive by itself. Without a patron, it dies and lives only from him: state, Church, business or a well-off private individual. If the patron loses interest in creation, it disappears.

Whence one immediately arrives at the definition of creation: it makes its way dying. Philosophy willingly distinguishes nature and culture, let's finally understand why. Always in the process of being born, nature is opposed to whatever does not cease to lose its strength, while culture fights for its existence and dies from creating. Such an accurate and profound definition that if, by chance, you encounter creation, here or there, powerful, rich, honored, fulfilled, dominant, and fat, you haven't found it, but rather its simulacrum or its counterfeit. In good health if it does not create, giving its life on the contrary to do so. You will recognize it from this sign that cannot fool you: an irremediable loss. Creative culture is this fragile child expiring among us, a new born in the throes of death ever since the world began.

And yet, it survives. Better, we know Maecenas only through the one who found shelter for his own immortality as it was being born, in Maecenas's home. The delicate child delivers from historical death the fortunate mortal who saves him. Not only does creation survive, but there is no long duration or even history except through this child, who alone holds the secret of subsistence.

Here are the donor and the beneficiary: the former certainly makes the latter live, and the latter, improbably, makes the former survive. It is useless to define the generous one without the recepient or the latter without the former, because they form an inseparable couple. Bound, in fact and by law, by the gift, but in an asymmetrical manner, one plays for the long term and the second for the short, the latter certain of making his mark and the former taking the riskiest chances.

Virgil assuredly lived thanks to Maecenas and La Fontaine thanks to Fouquet, but the probability of Maecenas and Fouquet surviving in history thanks to the fable and the epic is very low. In the couple thus united and stable in time, for the common and the rare, one operates in the present moment and as in real time, while the other hopes for continuity over the long run.

Which one and how?

In fact, the couple, together, risks the short term, a sure thing, for the long term, beyond all hope. In the face of their bond and common wager, death then appears, either individual and bodily, or collective, in the neglect of future generations. They fight in concert against two kinds of effacement.

De facto, would not this couple illuminate history, since it composes the two-faced prosopopoeia of its conditions: here fortune and there genius in the best cases, one unlocatable and the other rarer still: there, generosity; here, creation, one unusual, the second more exceptional still?

Here then are culture and economics, here their bond is realized, as gift and countergift *[contre-don]:* what a crucial experience, which allows us to observe the elementary conditions of history in a single example, and oh marvel, to decide between them!

Formerly and not long ago, certain people posited economics as the infrastructure of history, whereas we see that economics is merely its immediate condition. Whereas economics breaks time up into short periods, culture, which cannot be exhausted by time, furnishes the only and long-standing infrastructure, because it and it alone, through its weakness, has the strength to last.

Whence a new question: how is that what among us is revealed as the weakest, even childish and dying, in a state of irremediable loss, remains and lasts, stubborn, invariant, when our bodies are corrupted, our goods and our powers are effaced from the surface of the earth? How is it that creative culture founds the long term of history and its continuity, that, paradoxically, software founds and conditions hardware? The hardware founds the software, for the immediate present, but from then on the short term cedes its place to long duration, the relation is inverted: the hard *[dur]* is not durable, only the softest endures *[perdure]*.

But first of all, why this mothering, by the rich institution or man, of this soft, weak, and dying child? How can one explain the improbable generosity—aside from tax deductions? It is that fortune, left to itself, tends to reproduce an accrued fortune constrained to think only of itself, because command only knows how to engender hierarchy, war gives birth only to conflict and competition to rivalry; finally, these laws that enchain the monotonous time of history through identical reproductions make even the thickest-skinned blasé. Nothing new beneath this golden sun. What can be paid for becomes boring quickly. Buy ten houses then, dominate fifty shoe-shiners, wear twenty expensive rings, settle into some important position, what interest is there in conquering yet another one? You will never find anything but the same one, pretty much. Ease chews on repetition out of boredom, and the will to power, though infinite, has never produced anything but the unhappiness of men, and it encounters nothing but repugnant obedience, a relation that takes us back to the level of animals. They eat at the zoo, the great of this world. Whence the search for a good other than gold or domination, producers only of monotony.

Once again, what is creative culture? Often, in the morning, Maecenas would receive Virgil, who would read out loud to him what he had written the night before, both of them suddenly living this novelty. Creation invents news by recounting today what it didn't know yesterday—my vocation consists of writing and saying not what I know, boring, dead, and past, more than perfect, pluperfect, but, on the contrary, what I don't know and will astonish me—and the patron would run at dawn to the news, not toward the news that shouts every day at our broken ears of other murders that are really the same ones, of other scandals, wars, catastrophes, seizures of power, still and always the same, old monotonous repetitions of a world given over to iterative domination, but precisely toward the unforeseen of the artist, the unexpected and, strictly, the improbable.

Neither Maecenas nor especially Virgil knew the day before what would be said on the morrow.

In all epochs, this couple has produced a new epoch. Creative culture lives in the new and can define itself: as the lowest probability, thus irremediable loss, the greatest rarity. Nothing less monotonous or more inestimably precious: always at the stage of being born.

The old French language, in this regard more vivacious and robust than the one we have since used, called this producer of improbable novelty a finder: trouvère in the North, troubadour in the South. Alas! we no longer recognize anything but seekers or researchers. The creator does not seek; hell, he finds and if he does not find, what is he doing here, polluting culture with his resentments *[ressentiments]*?

This unpredictable invention is called peace, which follows from invention and conditions it. Peace, but also life.

The patron makes the artist live in the world opposite from the one in which the artist makes the patron survive. I want survival to signify not only prolonging existence, but also transfiguring it. In the realm of bread and water that the generous person gives to the creator, time goes from left to right, from birth to normal death, toward the greatest probability, the unique certainty of the end; in the other world created by the work that the finder gives back to the donor, time goes from right to left, from death to birth, toward the improbable, the greatest rarity, the astonishing novelty. The artist and the patron meet at the intersection of these two kinds of time.

This is why I said, The child. The creator, dying, goes toward birth and childhood, in the other direction of time. This is why the work does not use itself up and resists the monotony of history, whose flow runs toward the greatest probabilities of power, of glory, and of death. Going toward childhood and birth, it is always in the process of being born, just like the georgic and bucolic nature whose parturition Virgil announced to Maecenas every morning. That's how culture becomes a second nature.

The creator is born old and dies young, the opposite of those who are realistic and, as they say, have their feet on the ground, know how to be born infants and die senile like everyone else. The latter gives to the former the passing day, and the former gives him inexhaustible youth in return.

These two worlds that turn in two different directions and these two times know nothing of each other and rarely appreciate each other. The only improbable thing they have in common is this contingent couple united by the gift.

It is as difficult to receive as to give, because all cultures require, explicitly or tacitly, a countergift. I prefer to call it a pardon. What does the parasite give to the one who keeps him, who offers him a coat, a roof, and dinner? Vain words, hot air—things that are worthless, but which, for all that, cannot be bought.

So exchange ends up unbalanced: all against nothing; that is the one-sided contract. Or, it ends up in the gap between material and information. The situation is thus redressed, as one advances into modernity, where we have learned to value information, which theory defines as improbability, the greatest rarity.

But there is ordinary information and rare information. The whole question thus comes down to what I would call the risk of rarity. For a rare gift, a countergift can hardly be found: one encounters few patrons, certainly, but even fewer creators.

The search for the greatest effect will then, with certainty, make every patron's enterprise fail: what makes the most noise always follows the climate of its time and couldn't precede it; what announces a new time always arrives like a subtle breath of wind, softly, without great fanfare.

Whence this dangerous result: the properly cultural interest, powerfully creative, is often—not always—inversely proportional to the passions of the moment and sometimes, not always, corresponds to what holds no interest. This analysis holds as much for the work of art as for scientific research: it has happened that all funding is denied to some physicist seemingly engaged in investigations of no consequence who, ten years later, receives the Nobel Prize for an unequaled invention, in that very domain. There is no guarantee or insurance for creativity; but, inversely, once it succeeds, it reimburses the donor—who may even be dead by then—for the guarantee and the insurance a thousand times over, for a long time to come.

Thus the countergift goes back to a bet almost always lost but which yields infinitely—more than any other—if won. This gain can be defined very rigorously as that of survivor's insurance, for it concerns another life, a life transfigured that I have a tendency to consider as the only one that is livable, because what's at stake is immortality; through it, I return to the continuity of history. Virgil rendered Maecenas immortal and will carry him in his wake as long as humanity survives, while ten thousand patrons saved one hundred thousand bad rhymers from the famine they abundantly deserved.

But what does fame matter! All that matters is the fabric of history that it shows and constitutes. That is why I called the couple into which Virgil entered "generative."

Along the continuity thus woven, let us come to our era. Deterministic processes now furnish the so-called consumer society with products whose value often melts away in a lightning interval: nine-tenths, in volume and in weight, of what we have just bought at the supermarket goes directly into the trash to join the newspaper and almost all of what we received in the mail the same day. Consumerism or consumption denote this quick drift of value. Thus, the more a country, today, prospers and develops, the faster it leads us from schlock to rubbish. Of an object in circulation, ask yourself at what price you will have to sell it off tomorrow or in five years. We are losing rarity, and thus the long term, for these very reasons and at the same time.

The Roman Empire lasted two thousand years, the Middle Ages of Christianity a millennium, the British dominion over the world less than one hundred; the American reign began with the last war and started its decline a decade ago; how long will the five tigers of Asia govern? Our thinking should place patronage in the midst of the real conditions that history and economics create for value. Value is eroding in proportion to the speed of circulations: both are growing exponentially. Whence these diminishing returns.

I propose that one keep the appellation of patron for pure cultural assistance, for gifts accorded to those that contemporary society, neither less nor more than the preceding ones, always deprives of every good, to the point of death, and to call promotion or, worse, sponsorship, the gifts that, through rapid exchange, come around as advertising, as proper names on advertising banners, for sports or science, activities that are noble but almost as rich as the donors, since, through innovation, research precedes and pilots the economy itself. Even in real time the countergift surpasses the gift when the yacht wins the race or a discovery gets once-exhausted production going again. In this moment of quick drift toward schlock, advertising, an informational countergift, often costs more money than the vile product it insolently vaunts.

A gift with a minimal countergift, that is patronage. Only this minimum swims upstream, against the powerful current in which rarity is being lost. The French words *gré* [taste, liking], *grâce* [grace], or *gratuité* [gratuitousness], express this simple arrow of exchange without expecting or demanding a return. The logic of taste differs from that of exchange. Exchange is deterministic; it follows the rapid circulation and the lightning-fast drop that I have just evoked. Taste waits and plays for rarity. Exchange calculates and seeks to win; the free gift plays at winner-takes-nothing and loser-takes-all.

The rule of patronage strongly resembles the one that I follow in my daily work, the one that all research respects, the one that leads to all finds. Here it is: whoever wants to save his soul accepts that he may lose it, and if you only want to save it, you will certainly lose it. A winning formula that is the inverse of prudence, which strains toward power and glory. The one fights in exchange, and the other throws itself into the gift and its pure hazards. From these two different playing fields, suddenly two times will be born and branch off.

The patron happens upon Abbé Delille, a bad rhymer, or on Virgil, immortal, on a Sunday painter or on Braque or Raphael. The number of geniuses dying in desperation compared to the number of distinguished impotents shows that the choice, a difficult one, is comparable to a lottery, from which this rarity that we have lost will be drawn. The random search for such an improbability, with maximum information, seems to me the current role and the positive work of the patron, who thus restores to our world, devoured by banality, the forgotten improbable.

Thus, stochastically, the gift can be reversed: the payer reimburses with play money, with rapidly eroded value, a work that lasts transhistorically. And the patron keeps his name only through the artist. Whether by chance or lottery, the countergift is worth more than the gift, infinitely more.

This reversal of exchange and of taste inverts time itself, which, instead of wearing down or eroding value, makes it grow exponentially. Question: What appears today, in this time without culture and with almost no creation, to be the only value that resists all inflation and that, on the contrary, increases? Experts unanimously responded: the authentic work of art. What I wanted to prove.

But for authenticity in real time, here and now, you will find no expertise. Work then and take risks: a lottery for the audacious on whom, it is said, true fortune sometimes smiles.

I imagine that Virgil, one fine morning, recited before Maecenas the page of his poem where Aeneas descends to the Underworld. When silence replaced the music of the distich, the minister asked if it was necessary for the hero to die in order to enter the other world.

"And, in that case," he added, "how did he get out of there? Do you think he rose from the dead?"

"I don't know," Virgil answered, "if he died or didn't die from this blow, but, assuredly, this terrible risk in this infernal visit conditions the existence and the beauty of works. There is no real creation without such a voyage into the darkest tunnels."

"Explain what you mean then!" Maecenas cried out, in anguish.

"The one who comes out of the shadows, how, I don't know," the author of *The Aeneid* resumed, "call him Aeneas, as I did, or Homer maybe, whom I recall here and whose *Odyssey* made Ulysses descend to the same places.

"We evoke their shade through the magic of rhythm: Aeneas finally pulls himself from the abyss, Homer comes out, Ulysses too and Orpheus as well, and before them their millennarian ancestor, the archaic Gilgamesh, who was the very first one, in the fertile crescent, in our memory at least, to leave light-footed in quest of immortality. From the black box into which they decided to sink one day, they were delivered, one after the other, finally inoculated against forgetting, reborn, resurrected, the only true immortals by reason of their torment. Here is how, through heroic re-creation, culture becomes a second nature, the true one, the one that understands what it is to be born, that is, to truly come out of nothingness.

"Only the beautiful work takes us back to youth, and beauty alone calls humanity to its living, always re-created, present."

"But," questioned the minister, "what does this scene or this multiple series mean, what is meant by this suite, parallel to the history of our knowledge, this long procession of illustrious names displayed before Aeneas in the centuries of centuries, Gilgamesh, Orpheus, Ulysses, without forgetting Hercules and Theseus, a demigod who, not in history but according to legend, also ventured in these unnameable subterranean realms?"

"That if humankind does not fear death as a whole and its history," said Virgil with passion, "it owes this to the rare heroes who braved it up close in order to come back and join the generations to one another. One can call them our ferrymen: in the same way that each of us crosses the channel of sex so that children will awaken after we disappear. Just as love weaves our local and individual bond, body to body and in genetics, art accomplishes this transmission for the longest duration, with the acceptance of a personal death that founds history just as the acceptance of our death conditions the birth of our descendants.

"We feel alive and together, in time, via the beautiful work and in it, the one that integrates all knowledge, on the one hand, and that, on the other, does not fear to confront evil, pain, injustice, and death face to face."

Maecenas, standing, enthused by this farseeing projection, inquires then:

"But after us? After you, who extracts this memorable page from nothingness?"

"I imagine," resumed Virgil, "and I hope or prophesy that the ferrying does not stop; who knows if the future will see the advent of a religion—that diligent enthusiasm which resists negligence—founded in part on this idea that no one ever creates if he does not put himself in the gravest danger; it would be incarnated in a man who could be said to be divine and who would be reborn after having accepted death at the hand of the most powerful of his contemporaries.

"After him, works of music, painting, poems, statues will celebrate for millennia his resurrection, which will begin the history of their era, that of the good tidings that consist of placing our death, no longer before us, as something to be suffered, but finally, behind us, truly forgotten. Because he, too, will emerge from the Underworld.

"I dream of a genius, to be born in Italy, not far from here, who, later, will make me descend with him into these abominable places, accompanied by a woman so happy to be on this voyage that she will be called Beatrice. I will help him to enter, one more time, madly, then to emerge as the originator of a beautiful work. No," he added dreamily, "I cannot conceive that this heroic suite will stop.

"Our fundamental history follows that of the predecessors who show us radical necessity and the most difficult path. Art emerges from the tomb. If the seed does not die, it does not bring forth beautiful fruit.

"I tell you nothing more than a law of life: but the laws of the longest life are not like those of the shortest, that of our exhausted bodies. Doubtless, there exists in living flesh a program for this law; I write in my language, with these few others, the charter of history."

And finally Virgil fell silent.

Who succeeds him? In our museums, crowds commemorate the resurrection of Van Gogh or Gauguin, who died of poverty and hunger, deprived of any assistance, and celebrate these formidably present, living people with more press and fervor than the mighty who chased after glory—the wealthy, the powerful, the conquerors, or those decapitated amid the drumrolls of power—who are poor in works and in posterity. Without formulating it, posterity knows that it descends, to be sure, from revolutionaries or generals, but even more from an indigent lost in the archipelagoes of the Pacific, like Jean Valjean, who got lost in the sewers of Paris, in search of the same beauty as the one aroused by these names and these bodies that withstood time.

And we do not know the name of the unfortunate who, at this very moment, is giving his life to the work that our grandchildren will consume to survive: because if the appetite for bread is sometimes calmed, this hunger, I hope, will never be sated. What is culture finally? The irregular and regular resurrection of those who braved death to create, who return to join the tradition of yesterday to the vivacity of today. Without them, no continuity, no immortality of the human species, without their rebirth no history.

Who, then, should be called a patron? At the juncture where

long duration joins the brevity of life, in the rare places where history is projected on the moment, the moment pushes the tombstone so that a phantom is reborn or returns, the one who visits us today, just as Ulysses and Gilgamesh visited Maecenas through the voice of Virgil, just as Virgil visited Dante and gave him the golden bough, just as the shadow of Beatrice floated above us a moment, an evanescent phantom, barely recognizable, ready to be effaced in gusts of light air, but that alone, in these dark days, has the quality, generative vigor, and capacity to unite us in global human transmission and in the unexpected sowing of powerful creations.

Here it is, incandescent: begotten again by science and by the death of men; here it is, spirit, tongue of fire, seed of suns.

Education

The Law of the King: Nothing New under the Sun
Something New under the Sun, Elsewhere
Something New under the Sun, Here
Me. Night
You. Day
The Third Person: Fire

The Law of the King: Nothing New under the Sun
Temperature is but one variable of the climate of a place. A thousand other elements, linked to each other, change together there: relief and altitude, humidity, the thickness of the coat of arable land on the rocks, the richness and density of the flora or fauna . . . Local equilibria, stable or labile, sum up these factors. Let us suppose that one of these variables, temperature, decreases or strongly increases, is exacerbated for some reason.

Cold arrives and takes over: if it becomes terrifying, you could say that it reigns. Takes over and reigns. It does not moderately transform the fragile equilibrium obtained through the shimmering fusion of numerous factors, but kills or masks their diversity. Winter wins the battle: now king, it alone commands the winds, stops the waters, razes reliefs, covers the earth and seas, expels or makes the flora and fauna scarce, brings certain species to the fore, totally whitens spaces and volume: a single law vitrifies the expanse, nothing will ever be new beneath this faraway and frozen light, or the length of these pale plains. The monotony is not repeated before an indifferent eye, a source of light without a flame before which the new has disappeared. When uniformity appears, an all-powerful sun, absent or present, in fact, produced it.

Cold. Nothing new without sun.

If the opposite tendency takes hold, heat takes over, reigns, makes the space a desert, chases or starves animals and plants, covers the earth with sand and makes the waters of the sea evaporate, levels the hills and fills the valleys, dictates its unique law to the winds. With its burning, the flame destroys volume: in the expanse its order reigns.

The law of cold reigns in the countries of the North, that of the flame governs the South, nothing new with the sun or without it. The wisdom of Solomon places the sun so far away that it observes, detached, the dissolution that exposure to the sun, nonetheless, has produced. Does dissolution take place beneath its gaze? Certainly, but it occurs especially through its action. If the sun retreats, the white ice field advances, so that it cracks and the ochre desert extends in space. Conversely, when the new is lacking, seek, if you are not dead, the sun that makes the new absent itself.

Nothing new from the sun.

As proof, take temperate countries where the temperature is

115

milder, because dawn is oblique and twilight is extended in the modesty of the morning. All other factors reappear en masse: it is warm and cool, dry and humid, calm and windy, luminous, chiaroscuro; pines, palm trees, numerous fauna appear—everything becomes visible at once. The climate does not reach a peak, the space is not tied to a single excessive constraint. This variable mixture could be called time or weather *[temps]*, a word that signifies mixture or temperament and with which one qualifies the so-called temperate countries, which, for this reason, I guess, have in return invented history, I mean to say a temporal sequence—tempered, like a scale—of events.

Novelty occurs if the sun holds back.

If the waters hold back. With the rise in water level the flood begins and reigns, until everything is obliterated beneath the smoothness of the waters in mourning. Again, one law: marine transgression, reigning, swallows every detail beneath the flat level of the silky water.

If a species or a living variety holds back. Imagine the earth covered with billions of almost identical lizards or an interminable beach beneath a gray mass of crabs moving without a single gap, all prey to the exponential growth of reproduction. Or else space invaded by an inextricable network of interlacing creepers, a single family, or rats with a particular smell or ants with certain political customs. And these rats, these lizards, what will they eat when they have won the famous war for life, so that they will live only in an environment exclusively of rats or lizards? Lizards?

If man holds back. We arrange the world for ourselves alone, now exclusively political animals, inexorable winners of the war of survival, enclosed forever in the city built without limits, coextensive with the planet: already, who can leave the city called Japan or the greenhouse called Holland? When greenhouses cover the earth—disaster. In the midst of stones and glass, men will have nothing but glass and stones beneath them, for building, and, in front of them, for living, in a world finally vitrified, subjected to their law alone. Living from relations, eating, drinking only from their own bonds, finally dedicated to politics and to politics alone, finally alone, long creepers in knotted networks of communication, great colonies of agitated ants, lizards by the billions. The human species takes over and is going to reign, is not wary of itself, does not hold back, withholds neither its power nor its science nor its politics. The hominid must learn to hold back, must learn modesty and shame; and his language must learn understatement; his science, reserve. To persevere unceasingly in its being or in its power characterizes the physics of the inert and the instinct of animals.

Doubtless humanity begins with holding back.

If God holds back. God is the only being to whom such a thing has happened, already. Monotheism destroyed local gods, we no longer hear goddesses laugh amid the springs, nor do we see the genies appear in the foliage; God emptied the world, the great Pan, they say, is dead. When the sun appeared on the side of the Middle East, the stars paled; in the inferno of the unity the number of colors in the medley dissolved. Nothing can now lay claim to novelty beneath the torch of omnitude: a complete well of true thoughts, conditional and creative omnipotence, the preformation of everything that is possible, closure under the law—God does not hold back.

Wrong. God holds back throughout all eternity. Limited—can that be?—by the power of evil, therefore dual and trinitary, surrounded by multiple messengers, seraphims and archangels, powers and dominations, overburdened day after day with the small glory of men who have arrived at beatitude or saintliness, encumbered with martyrs, with virgins and the Virgin, God holds back or, of his own accord, holds back his power. The sacred history of God recounts something other than his solitude and shows, on the contrary, his holding back, his suspension, our freedoms. Whence his bonhomie, his tolerance, his sweetness . . . and if God did not adhere to a strict monotheism? What the devil, He created the world, and, consequently, a lot of people aspire to command.

Perhaps Satan shows the clemency of God. Maybe existing evil demonstrates God's goodness. Maybe the existence of bad demons—like that of angels and cherubs, of saints, of the holy family—good spirits and bad finally on the same level and for once and with the same function, maybe the existence of all these impediments—that God tolerates or that we impose on his ubiquity, including his own incarnation—sings to us of his benevolence and his divine mercy, of all the latitude that he gives. We have God to thank for having held back a good deal short of monotheism. We are perhaps surviving on this reserve. Perhaps God only created the world in the field of his abstention? How much weight would we have if he had not held back?

Moved by tradition, I believed for a long time that monotheism had killed local gods, and I cried for the loss of the hamadryads, a pagan like all peasants, my fathers. The solitude in which the trees, rivers, seas, and oceans found themselves tore me up, I dreamed of repeopling the empty space, I would have willingly prayed to the destroyed gods. I hated monotheism for this holocaust of deities, it seemed to me to be wholesale violence, without mercy or exception. One incapable of thinking in a new way, because linked to the millenarian battle of the gods, to this gigantomachy from which we make our model.

On the contrary, I see that God welcomes the gods, that he does not bring his arm down on the devil, because Satan, obviously, still takes all the powers of the world with no protests from God. I observe that he allows the angels to rag on him and the sweet crowd of saints to compete with him, that he even disappears a bit in the crush of wings, aureoles, and robes, that one can hardly distinguish him amid the palms. I discover that God is good and maybe even infinitely weak. He holds back with modesty and shame. Not long ago, he even allowed himself to be killed without reacting in any notable way. By the same token, I laugh at the old gigantomachy of small local gods, forever on the brink of war, like us. Already, I find myself less pagan.

A single, supposedly general law results from the frenzied expansion of a local element that loses its hold, if it ever had one, that forgets moderation, if it ever learned it, in view of making the remainder disappear.

Dawn effaces the stars, nothing in the sky will ever be new after it. Now the sun is nothing but a yellow dwarf, whose aurora hides the blue giants. And yet the supergiants continue to turn, the galaxies also. The dwarf has lost moderation and abandoned its self-restraint. And yet, the others turn. The expansion of the single law of a very small star is called the aurora.

By themselves, gases occupy the volume that is offered before their expansive pressure. No one has ever seen a gas show proof of restraint in order to leave a part of the space empty. Barbarism follows the single law. The law of expansion. That of gases. They propagate themselves. The barbarian spreads. Violence spreads blood, which spreads out. Pestilence, epidemics, microbes are propagated. Noise, ruckus, rumors spread. In the same way, force, power, kings spread. In the same way, ambition spreads. In the same way, advertising spreads. The rubric of all the things that spread, as amply as a gas, of all the things that expand, that take up space, that occupy volume, must be named. Evil gets around, that is its definition: it exceeds its limits.

Who, on the contrary, will sing of the modesty of culture, of the shame of truth, of the understatement of beautiful language, of the wisdom of restraint? The excellent quality fades and is lacking: there is no beautiful décolleté without defects in the shoulder. The lacks and defects required by truth, beauty, goodness, certainly, but also by life.

We owe life to the restraint of God, created as we were in the margins of his restraint. We also owe life to the all the gaps left by the other living things, the Earth, the atmosphere, the waters, and the flames that, in return, owe their existence to the marginal reserves that we leave them.

Death always lays down the law; thus birth hides its stable in the margins of nonlaw. Nature is in retreat.

Nothing new is born if some intensified sun stops it.

The work is born in a reserved hollow.

Morality demands this abstention first of all. First obligation: reserve. First maxim: before doing good, avoid the bad. To abstain from all evil, simply hold back. Because in expanding, good itself, just like the sun, very quickly becomes evil. This first obligation conditions life, creates a readiness for a sense of emergence from which novelty will come.

The new can be born in chiaroscuro.

The gentle man holds back. He reserves some strength to retain his strength, refuses in himself and around him the brute power that is propagated. The sage thus disobeys the single law of expansion, does not always persevere in his being and thinks that elevating his own conduct to a universal law is the definition of evil as much as madness.

Thus reason seeks not to submit to an empire, in particular that of its own expansion. It reserves some reason to retain its reason. The gentle and reasonable man can thus disobey reason, so that margins are born around him, to provide for novelty. He invents good tidings. Finder, troubadour.

If the sun, if the waters hold back, if the living species reserve their power, if we put the brakes on the expansion of our reasons. God abstained. If not, he would have been alone. As it is difficult to spot him in the dense crowd of saints and angels, whoever has found him still seeks him, fragmented still in the Trinity. He hides and allows himself to be invaded. His absence in space and in history signifies his restraint.

Good tidings are born at midnight: without sun.

We should conceal ourselves a bit beneath the trees and the rose bushes, open our politics to the rights of the world. We should hold back, each of us, abstain collectively especially, invest a part of our power in softening our power.

He is human who does not always bring his arm down on the weak, as a matter of course, or on the strong, out of resentment, or even on those proven to be bad. Humanity becomes human when it invents weakness—which is strongly positive.

To unceasingly persevere in one's being, to even go beyond one's completely developed perseverance, to overcome while preserving, this is the conduct of madness. Paranoia could be defined as the expansion of a local, exacerbated trait vitrifying mental space so as not to leave any chance of growth to another variable. When present, a psychotic eradicates all other presence, just as psychosis has leveled everything in him. Royal, imperial, solar, he perseveres in his being, expands, converts his entourage. The propagation of pathology overcomes everything that it finds before it and absorbs it while preserving itself. Nothing new under this madness.

We can hardly stand this psychosis when an individual imposes it on us, but when it becomes collective, we sometimes give our lives for it. Our social behaviors often translate maladies into giant models or add together a number of atoms or elements that, taken separately, are nothing but morbid. Madness, the great kind, always resembles, more or less, the conduct of someone who wants to become king and begins to identify himself with the sun. Common people are not mistaken when they say that the madman believes himself to be Napoleon. Now, it is never said that the one who believes this is mistaken. It had to happen that one day some Corsican math student would believe it up to the very end. The collective assembles and recognizes itself around the potentate who seeks to be taken for the real thing. If he succeeds, he is crowned emperor; if he fails, he is labeled a madman. The divide is rather narrow that separates the two decisive reckonings. Here, in any case, is a single variable that tries to spread beyond its little niche, that perseveres in its being or overcomes itself in preserving itself. To define madness, do not shrink from using the methodical words of philosophy.

Madness develops according to the same law of expansion as the one we wish for in the name of reason. Reason wants to invade the whole place just like any other variable, or any other insanity. Reasonable signifies holding back just short of the capacity of one's own reason, so that one calls reasonable the one who is neither always nor everywhere right and who does not take advantage of those who are never right or of those who, in extreme circumstances, can sometimes be right. There is a miniscule and close to zero probability that one will always be right about everything and everyone.

Thought begins when the desire to know is purged of any compulsion to dominate. Let us bring up our children in the shame of reason, so that they experience its modesty. Let us think of reason as ratio, proportion: it measures the quantity or the volume of an element mixed in a solution. How much water in this pure wine? The name that is also given to the coefficient of propagation in a suite or a series, reason (ratio) is clothed in proportion. One does not work without the other; no reason or proportion without mixtures—thus reasonable reason will laugh at pure reason, as it would at an oxymoron, so deeply does it plunge into mixed bodies, so fully does it teach that everything is not—and far from it—always and everywhere as it is reckoned to be. How can we have an expansive and united idea of reason that makes a madness of reason, that is the exact opposite of a proportion?

If reason holds back. Reason is born under the Greek name of *logos,* relation or proportion, as soon as Thales discovers, at the foot of the pyramids, that the big ones are equivalent to the small one, according to a common relation. Cheops and Khephren, formidable pharaohs, hold back for the first time, before Mykerinos, which itself holds back in the face of the upright, free, and proud body of the surveyor, whose mediocre size projects, beneath the sun, a shadow similar to the three enormous shadows according to the same ratio or reason. Plunged in darkness, outside the solar follies of kings, Thales invents science.

Here something new in the shadow of the sun.

Thus novelty arises at every minute of the day or night: this uninterrupted fecundity of time, unexpected in the dry and burning desert, we call the history of sciences, which equals that of reason's retentions.

If rational science holds back. We meticulously organize a world where only canonized knowledge will reign, a space that, up close, risks looking like an earth covered with rats. Unified, crazy, tragic, science takes over, will soon reign, just as winter reigns and takes over. Knowledge is certainly excellent, but in the same way cold is: when it remains cool. Science, assuredly, is just and useful, but the way heat is: if it remains mild. Who denies the utility of flame and ice? Science is good, who denies it, and even, I am sure, one thousand times better than a thousand other things that are also good, but if it claims that it is the only good and the whole good, and if it behaves as if this were the case, then it enters into a dynamic of madness. Science will become wise when it holds back from doing everything it can do.

As judicious as an idea appears to be, it becomes atrocious when it reigns alone. It would be dangerous if the hard sciences came to pass themselves off as the only way of thinking. Or of living. It is possible to conceive of the sciences becoming wise. It would be enough for them to learn understatement, reserve, holding back: the content of an idea matters a little less than the way it is put into practice, the value of science is esteemed as much for its performances as its truth—one judgment should temper another. Yes, what does the rigor or the depth of a theorem matter if it ends up killing men, or making an excessive power weigh on them?

Wisdom provides the yardstick of moderation. The fear of a unitary solution makes for the beginning of wisdom. No solution constitutes the only solution: neither a particular religion, nor a particular politics, nor a particular science. The only hope remains that science can learn a tolerant wisdom that the other instances of power were never really able to learn and prevent a united, madly logical, rationally tragic world.

Truth, by all rights, should not assume the right of spreading in space. Wisdom adds restraint to the true, reserve to the criteria of the true. Now, I would not judge as true what cannot or does not know how to hold back from conquest.

The madness of solar truth.

If science and if reason hold back, if philosophy holds back. I love philosophy because it carries in itself that word of love that I love, that wisdom that I discovered only late. I know nothing better than it, nothing larger, warmer, deeper, or more extensive, more luminous, nothing that renders one more intelligent, nothing that understands the things of the world better, that enables one to live better and to attain rare beauty. I have given it my life, my body, my time, my pleasures, my nights, and my adventures, even my loves; it took them from me and gave them back to me magnified. But, as surely as I love it, I know that it must not be promoted or given power, but, on the contrary, it must be kept from taking power. Too dangerous. Lover of philosophy, I would never become its zealot. I do nothing to spread its power.

Philosophy must beget men of work; I hope that it will be sterile in company men, in men of power. Sterile, an institution perseveres in its being, advances, blind and stubborn. The work—timid, weak, fragile, lost—waits for one to take it, shines softly like a pebble in a hollow, does not spread of its own accord, fortunately. By itself, the work holds back. There is something new in its chiaroscuro.

If philosophy, forgetful of the work, seizes power somewhere, it just as quickly reigns over cemeteries. History shows no counterexample. Too dangerous, philosophers. More terrifying than politicians, priests, and scientists, they multiply the risks of the others. Let us not grant power to ideas because they multiply the reach of power. Theories—too dangerous. As they expand in space, millions of men will soon march with cadenced footsteps thousands of miles from the place the theories were broadcast before gigantic portraits of those who promoted them. Single propagation and final solution. One always believes that an idea is not dangerous except when it is false. Let the idea express truth, in good time; let us spare it publicity.

The wisdom proper to philosophy comes from its restraint. If philosophy constructs a universalizing world, art frames it with a margin of reserved beauty. Philosophers, make your work with exactitude and suffer in silence that they call you poets—those who are ordinarily excluded from the city. It is better so. Construct a great work in which, precisely placed, are found the things of the world—rivers, oceans, constellations, the rigors of formal science, models, structures, neighborhoods, the approximate exactitudes of experimentation, turbulences or percolation, the fluctuations of history, crowds, time, small distances, the fables of language, and the narratives of the people—but construct it so beautifully that even its beauty holds it back. Holds it back in singularity. Defines it. Preserves it from excess. Happily and by definition, the inimitable does not find imitators and thus does not spread or propagate itself.

Altogether beautiful, altogether new.

The beautiful contains the true, I mean that it holds it back, limits its expansion, closes up the trail when it passes, forms its traits. The true demands a limit and asks the same of beauty.

When science and reason have attained beauty, we will no longer run a risk. Beautiful, philosophy brushes aside all danger.

Beautiful, the true forgets to advance in space. The beautiful is the true at peace with itself: the truth held back.

If language holds back. There is nothing, I truly know this, as beautiful, as secretly musical, as my language; no other language hides with as much discretion, is as precise and clear without showing off; no mode of expression approaches understatement more closely; there is nothing as pure as French taste, excellent, refined, surreptitious, as absent as God beneath the host of cherubs or as the lilac behind the pear and apple dried in an old Yquem; nothing approaches beauty as closely, yet I would not be able to bear having my language spoken everywhere and always.

I would suffer a lot, I think from speaking English today, that is to say as a mother tongue. Alas, it no longer holds back. Yet how beautiful it was!

When all the people of the world finally speak the same language and commune in the same message or the same norm of reason, we will descend, idiot imbeciles, lower than rats, more stupidly than lizards. The same maniacal language and science, the same repetitions of the same names in all latitudes—an earth covered with screeching parrots.

When the powerful and the rich no longer speak anything but English, they will discover that the language dominating the world lacks the term *modesty*. They will have abandoned, with derision, all other dialects to the poor.

If the strongest, if the best hold back. The free citizens of Athens, of Thebes, the Parisian revolutionaries of year II, the potentates of the West, today weighted down with dollars, invented or practice democracy, they say, whereas it served them or still serves them as publicity, or as a screen that hides the fact that they crushed the slaves and wogs, that they were going to take the place of the decapitated nobles or that they are exploiting the Third World to death.

"What is the best form of government?" theoreticians constantly ask. Put this way, the question dictates: aristocracy. The government of the best and the best form of government, the West has known nothing but this form since the dawn of its time.

Always and everywhere in our culture, aristocrats considered themselves equals, brothers in arms bound to the hard law of duels; equivalent fortunes in a savage competition, pitiless competitions between deserving experts. It is always necessary to form or imitate the ideal of man, that is to say, the best possible: born rich or intelligent. When one knows only by example and acts only from models, how can competition be avoided, that is to say, aristocracy and inequality?

Thus one tendency is optimized, chosen: arms, wealth, or merits grow, the race begins, in order for force or fortune or talent to occupy the terrain. Why would the best things hold back?

Yet we discover today this new but ancient fact: that the Earth cannot give to all its children what the rich tear from it today. There is scarcity.

While our constant aristocratic models increase or optimize a given tendency in order for it to invade space, true democracy, the one I hope for, diminishes or minimizes the same or said force. To enjoy power and not to pride oneself on it, here lies the beginning of wisdom. Of civilization.

The political philosophy of restraint, of holding back: the only thinkable equality now presupposes poverty—not as lack of wealth, but as a positive value.

The Third World precedes us.
Let's go.

Something New under the Sun, Elsewhere

During the battle of the Pacific, one of the harshest of the last world war, a large supply ship, whose name and flag I will conceal, sustained such a rain of torpedoes and projectiles that it shipped as much water as its tonnage. Yet it did not sink: it is possible for a ship to remain afloat in extreme conditions.

Without an engine or a rudder, deprived of all radio contact, suddenly enveloped by mist, seized by currents, then by winds when the fog rose, disabled, abandoned to meteors, unable to act, it wandered alone for two or three weeks on the deserted expanse of the sea, after having lost its squadron, which, believing it to have been at the bottom of the ocean for a long time, had ceased searching for it. Since the quickwork and deadwork had disappeared beneath the water, almost the entire crew occupied the heights, masts and rigging, to seek with all their eyes some sign on the horizon. The survivors recounted that in those moments they believed they had abandoned the world of men.

And all of a sudden, one beautiful morning, a miracle. Land ho! Illuminated by the rising sun, a coral barrier appears directly in front, enclosing a tranquil lagoon of green waters from which a long, flat rib of sand emerges, behind which high cliffs are covered in a plumage of palm trees and waterfalls. One would have thought it one of the Cocos Islands, the most beautiful and the most typical of the Pacific lands, but situated thousands of miles further east.

The tranquil swell pushed the ship, with all hands and its cargo, toward the first rocky point, where it smashed and foundered in two minutes, as if it had waited twenty days, in equilibrium, for this lightning moment. But the rafts and the whaling boats, put to sea much earlier, carried to the river's edge sailors and officers in the starved disorder that is easily imagined and in the mad hope of surviving. Not one drowned.

Then from all points along the coast come long canoes garnished with rowers and heralds who hail them with a great many cries and gestures, songs, drums. Each rescue boat finds itself besieged.

Since the sailors understand nothing of these demonstrations, they cannot decide what to do: to defend themselves before an attack or to embrace those who welcome them.

Suddenly silence descends: the chief or king appears, almost naked, majestic, asks for the captain. The latter gets up, confronts the splendor. Enchantment descends on the scene. The natives turn their small boats around, head in the other direction, and lead those who suddenly become their guests toward land.

For long months nothing was lacking for the complete happiness of the shipwrecked. The survivors recounted that at these moments they believed they had landed in paradise on earth. Exchanges that fully satsified the parties, games and laughs, delicious feasts around those Polynesian ovens hollowed out of the earth and from which the cooks took sumptuous pancakes made of sweet potatoes. Certain of the men, as in previous centuries, took a wife, others cleared a corner for a garden in which to sow some seeds saved from the disaster.

Once these matters of living were settled, interminable discussions began—about each other's gods, whose performances they compared, about the rules followed in given matters by each of the two communities, their advantages and disadvantages—first through obliging gestures, then in a progressively clear and mastered language.

The natives nourished a strange passion for words: they asked for the precise translation of their terms and were tireless in their explanations. The assemblies multiplied and never ended—so many were the jokes and so great the good humor. It was necessary to speak of love, religion, rites, police, and work, in the greatest detail. They wore themselves out on parallels: the constraints differed, but each was subjected in his country to equally complicated rules, incomprehensible to the point of laughter to his interlocutors, but on neither side were these rules neglected. In brief, beneath very spectacular differences, all ended up recognizing many resemblances, and that brought them closer together.

Time passed, nothing appeared on the horizon. For the natives, nothing ever had. The elders recounted nevertheless what their elders had recounted, and so on: that in distant times pale populations had landed there, but never since. As for those aboard the war vessel, they did not remember that an island existed on their maps with this particular bearing.

Some of them called it Nil Island, but, because they were no longer divided for services, as they had been on board, into port-siders and starboarders, others began, for fun, to call this blessed land Third Island, like an immobile small boat with an undivided crew. Time passed.

Because they risked becoming bored, even in making comparisons, despite a sense of happiness and satiety, they organized soccer tournaments. Initially spectators of these games or fights (for which the feasts unfolded on taboo terrains), the talented islanders quickly learned, barefoot, to direct a ball while running, to defend and attack, to multiply the passes, and to shoot for the goal. Their goalies especially were given to very extravagant acrobatics. Matches followed in which sometimes separate teams within each community faced off and sometimes the islanders faced their hosts. In the huts, in the evening, strategies and training were debated over root beer. Time took refuge in these matches. The survivors recounted that during them they lost all memory of their former life.

Which nonetheless returned, one beautiful evening, in the form of an aircraft carrier that suddenly appeared without anyone ever having seen it leave from any point on the horizon. One even said that its whaling boat touched land before it had been noticed, having dropped both gigantic anchors in front of the coral reef. The admiral commanding the ship summoned the captain on board and decided to repatriate right away this fine society that no longer planned on anything but soccer in the tropics, paradise, and a dream life. Separations, tears, desperation on both sides, pathetic farewells, promises, gifts, songs, and threnodies, the sailors of the aircraft carrier, at attention the length of the gangway, at the ready to cast off, could not believe their ears or their eyes. The anchor was lifted to the sound of the melancholic bugle-call, the cliffs and the waterfalls disappeared in the circle of the sea.

Each one on his own, in some new unit, resumed hostilities, the Admiralty having taken great care to disperse the group. Some of them died, others didn't, as chance would have it. Then the war ended, as we know, at Hiroshima. End of the first act.

The second and last act begins in a city of the Western world, whose name and language I will conceal. Two of the survivors find each other there, by chance, in a bar, a church, or a market, who knows, doubtless at the exit to a stadium. They clap each other heartily on the back, evoke old combats, and soon bring up the paradise lost. One survivor, the more enthusiastic, suggests going back. Why not? says the other. Each one seeks their old mates, finds some of them, now somewhat dispersed in society, space, and fortune. In short, the wealthy pay less than the poor, and the voyage is organized. When there is no regular line from one place in the world to another, one must certainly charter a small boat . . .

. . . whose smallness surprises the natives; they have never seen anything but enormous aircraft carriers—except the hull filled with water whose remains had so quickly sunk.

The triumph of return: new delicious feasts around the same ovens, exchanges that always delight the parties, songs and threnodies, broken by exclamations: that the king has grown older, how the girls and boys have grown; but the women remain beautiful and one must go kneel at the tomb of the dead one knew and who have not had the chance to see those who have returned. All this done but especially said, the leisure activities resume and everyone returns, en masse, to the stadium, led by the aging king. Everyone takes his place and the clamor rises.

The match opposes the eastern team to the western one, two towns on the island. Superb, dramatic, elegant, it ends with the score of three to one, at the end of twenty-four minutes. The sailors then get up to leave the spectacle and return to sleep. It is evening. "But no, but no," the crowd clamors, and makes them sit down again, "it is not finished."

The game resumes even more beautifully and, beneath live torches, extends into the night. Time passes and the old sailors no longer understand: exhausted, out of breath, the players fall one after the other, legs devoured by cramps. But, stubborn, the match continues. Each team scores, and, toward the small hours of dawn, the score is eight to seven. It's becoming tedious.

All of a sudden, the populace rises, waves their arms and hands, everything is at an end: the goal of equality has just been shot point blank by a forward who is carried in triumph around the playing field. Each one cries: eight to eight, eight to eight, eight to eight! Sleepy, stunned, incapable of clearly grasping the event, the sailors hastily return to their cabins to go to sleep.

A few hours later, the endless discussion is continued. Strategy, tournament, scores, previous conversations are resumed. And little by little the truth comes to light.

The natives played the same game as before, with teams consisting of the same number of men on playing fields in the same shape, but they had changed a rule, one single small rule.

"A game is finished when a team wins and the other loses, and only in that case!" say our sailors. "You must have a conqueror and a conquered."

"No, no," claim the islanders.

"How then do you decide between your teams?" ask the sailors.

"What does that word mean in your dialect?"

"A difference in goals."

"We do not understand your ideas. When you cut up a pancake according to the number of those that are seated around the fire, don't you share it?"

"Certainly."

"And each eats a piece, right?"

"Surely."

"This pancake, did it occur to you not to share it?"

"That wouldn't mean anything," the sailors protest in turn, the portsiders or starboarders of always.

"But yes, as in soccer. Someone will eat the whole thing and the others won't eat anything, if you don't share it."

The pale, stunned faces are quiet.

"Why would you decide between the teams?"

" . . ."

"We do not understand that which is neither just nor human, because one gets the upper hand. So we play the game for the time that you taught us. If at the end the result is nil, the game ends on true sharing.

" . . ."

"If not, the two teams, as you say, are decided between, which is something unjust and barbaric. What is the point in humiliating the vanquished if one wishes to pass for civilized like yourselves?

So, one must begin again, for a long time, until sharing returns. Sometimes the game lasts for weeks. Some players have even died from it."

"Died from it? Really?"

"Why not?"

" . . ."

"So the western town is happy and has a fête, as does the eastern town, as well as the northern and southern towns. The feasts, which the game of sharing interrupts for a time, sometimes a long time, can resume around the ovens from which the pancakes are taken."

In the winds that led them back to their city and their family, amid the regular rocking of the hammocks, in sweet equilibrium in the crib of the hold, the sailors dreamed of this singular land, a third or nil island, missing from maritime maps. They continued to chew things over, in bed, their hands behind their heads:

"Say, the last war, we won it, right?"

"Certainly."

"At Hiroshima?"

" . . ."

"Truly won it?"

"Are you trying to determine the true conquerors?" the second threw out, who was passing by the gangway, "I know them well, from having taken them sometimes in my boat . . . Ethnologists, sociologists, I don't know their title, but they study the natives of the islands . . . and in general take men for the subject of studies, that is, for objects."

"They sing of victory: who can conceivably be above those who explain and understand others who, from this point of view, will never again be their fellow creatures, what is more their neighbors?"

Something New under the Sun, Here

But he—scribe, learned man, legislator—desiring to justify himself, said to Jesus, "And who is my neighbor?"

Jesus replied, "A man was going down from Jerusalem to Jericho, and he fell among robbers, who stripped him and beat him, and departed, leaving him half dead. Now by chance a priest was going down that road; and when he saw him he passed by on the other side. So likewise a Levite, when he came to the place and saw him, passed by on the other side. But a Samaritan, as he journeyed, came to where he was; and when he saw him, he had compassion, and went to him and bound up his wounds, pouring on oil and wine; then he set him on his own beast and brought him to an inn, and took care of him. And the next day he took out two denarii and gave them to the innkeeper, saying, 'Take care of him; and whatever more you spend, I will repay you when I come back.' Which of these three, do you think proved neighbor to the man who fell among the robbers?"

The legislator responded:

"The one who showed mercy on him."

The Gospel according to Saint Luke 10:29–37

The bell rings. The door of the classroom opens for the school children onto an empty and ugly courtyard that they invade screaming during the so-called recreation period; from the beginning, in our latitudes, a judicial division of space and time is offered to or imposed on human offspring, who are split into groups in order to build their reflexes. Inside, the great stature of the teacher dictating spelling and arithmetic ensures the order of the rows and benches, classification; beyond the threshold, outside, the quarreling spreads cries and furor, battles, hopeless chaos as soon as the bell rings.

A child of the people, of the streets, and of the countryside, I spent my childhood or hell in the schoolyard, in terror of ambushes and relentless vengeance by gangs led by young, arrogant, and pugnacious murderers, cocks, or dukes. It was enough for them to have an advantage of three inches in height to be able, unchallenged, to throw off balance—from the thigh, the shoulders or the ankle—whoever was not attacking them. In the inner courtyard, between the tree trunks, along the repulsive outhouses, in clouds of dust, a jungle or primitive forest, the strongest relentlessly tortured the weakest, for pure pleasure, and the blows always beat down on the same ones without respite. But the most muscular or vociferous did not carry the day for long if he did not recruit around him a guard, more powerful together than any duke, even more aggressive and roguish than the first cock. Whence the contemporary formation of a rival militia at the orders of a new enemy, thus furnished with bodyguards or ministers. The battles between gangs begin, as soon as the bell rings.

I remember very lucidly that I was less disgusted by the young chiefs, proud of their biceps, than by those lieutenants, salivating with servile obedience, seeking power without having the means, secondhand executioners, henchmen so much more implacable toward the humble and anonymous troop, who were peaceful but bent beneath the wind of power. These adjuncts were doubtless mimicking their parents: we were living that ignoble era during which France lost its soul in collaborating with the Nazis. No recess ended without the bell announcing some ignominy.

Adults give the name "playground accidents," which are covered under insurance plans, to the veritable crimes knowingly perpetrated, in the seeming turbulence of games, by irresponsible legal minors. The following bell thus rang the hour of vengeance or of revenge, as was said in the newspapers in regard to the grown-up war, a battle prepared by the hostile camp by means of signs and messages circulating through the classroom from hand to hand under the desks, beneath the paternal and blind gaze of the instructor. The general roar when the door opened after the bell, which adults think expresses the fully legitimate relief of finally leaving behind the white notebooks and the blackboard, simply signifies the reopening of hostilities.

When I hear the vibrating bell that chimes the hours in so-called institutions of learning, I know that it trembles with terror.

At home, civil and familial time had the same rhythm: bombing sirens, various alerts, the news announcing, hour after hour, after the theme song, the opening of new killing fields. Between the Spanish revolution of 1936, the Second World War and its summing up at Hiroshima, what child would have perceived the difference between these giant massacres and the merciless vendettas that brought together the cubs, the sons of wolves, and the future fathers of the same through the eternal return of the same signal marking time, the doleful law of our history writ small or large, the reflex bell of dogs?

The bell finally rings. Who would not have savored the silent repose and a certain air of paradise in the classroom when the door barred the storms of the schoolyard and the good schoolmaster dictated two quatrains on the idyllic wine-harvesting in which the author had surely taken no part, since the bickering ceased neither around the vines heavy with blue fruit nor in the winepress where the sexes were cruelly thrown together: what in poems one calls the calm happiness of the bucolic? For a long time I believed, at least until I was nine, in the ideal peace of the intellect, in pastorals, in the utopia of figures and numbers, until the moment, seven times blessed, when I suddenly understood that I liked them because the schoolmaster singled me out as first in the class and shielded me with his shadow: on this side of the wall, I thus found myself beneath the same wind possessing another kind of power, hard and roguish, a cock and thus pugnacious, a gang leader . . . Horror, ignoble disgust, already divining servile gleams in certain looks and in the arching of backs. A shame took hold of me that never abated, a secret passion that pushes me to speak now of ourselves, of our speculative schemes and of their essential unhappiness, hidden in another space, an intellectual utopia, and separated in time by some sonorous indicator.

I have passed enough of my life on warships and in lecture halls to testify before youth, which already knows, that there is no difference between the purely animal or hierarchical customs of the playground, military tactics, and academic conduct: the same terror reigns in the covered playground, in front of torpedo launchers, and on campus, this fear that can pass for the fundamental passion of intellectual workers, in the majestic shape of absolute knowledge, this phantom standing behind those who write at their table. I sense it and divine it, stinking, slimy, bestial, returning as regularly as the bell rang, opening and closing colloquia where eloquence vociferates in order to terrify speakers all around.

Far from bringing us closer to peace, science and intelligence distance us from it even more than do muscle, shouting, or size. Culture continues war by other means—by the same means, maybe. In theoretical gangs one encounters the same little chiefs, in effect, the same lieutenants, drooling in servile obedience and similar peaceful legions, humbly bent beneath the wind of power that they sometimes take for fashion, worse, more often for truth. To call the site of universities a campus, what literal luck, since this word formerly designated the entrenched camp set up in the evening by Roman soldiers before an attack or for defense. In effect, the experts know to which faction, to which gang a given campus belongs and what pressure group holds court there.

Now the intellectual, linguistic, theoretical, knowing means of conducting a war cannot be compared to the blows of the cock and the duke of the schoolyard: they are finer, slier, more global, more transparent, and include the innocent irresponsibility of pure speculation. The strongest boxer in the world never fells anything but a pitiable body with his swing or his uppercut, and seems to me a saint of paradise next to the theoretical physicist whose equation can blow up the Earth or the philosopher who enslaves entire peoples for generations—or the sect that mimics him throughout his career. Today we have produced philosophies that are so global they eradicate all history and close off the future, such powerful strategies they achieve the same deterrence as the atomic weapon and result in perfectly efficacious cultural genocide.

Here is the unhappiness proper to our work: like a coefficient, intelligence multiplies vengeance as much as can be desired and pretends to annul it by dissimulating. As vindictively as it acts, violence grows little and slowly when fists and feet are involved, but it skyrockets and invades time and history as soon as reason takes command.

Thus traditional political theories, just like current strategic games, gravely overvalue the pacificatory role of rational knowledge: this miscalculation constitutes the self-publicity of these disciplines. Reason always lurks around proportion and dominance. It thus throws up a bridge between the classroom and the so-called playground.

Why, on the contrary, does philosophy hold on to being called so? Because it does not ask us to love either intelligence, knowledge, or reason, but Sophia, wisdom. What wisdom?

Pacified knowledge.

Without knowing it, knowledge is committed to a risky career—for us, the learned, as well as for others—a danger we only discover in moments of tension or crisis. A postwar French university philosopher, I uneasily survived ten diverse terrors maintained by theoreticians who were serfs to political or academic ideologies, cocks and dukes once again, director-princes of groups controlling beneath their pressure the space of the campus, appointments, and footnotes, forbidding all freedom of thought at all cost. I do not hold any particular individual or sect responsible for these terrors, since that would amount to getting revenge; I blame the very functioning of intelligence in the institution and of the latter in the former, the reciprocal involvement of science and society.

Thus, out of regard for the health of life and mind, I had to conceive, for my private use, some rules of ethics or deontology:

After attentive examination, adopt no idea that would contain, on the face of it, any trace of vengeance. Hatred, sometimes, takes the place of thought but always makes it smaller;

Never throw yourself into a polemic;

Always avoid all membership: flee not only all pressure groups but also all defined disciplines of knowledge, whether a local and learned campus in the global and societal battle or a sectorial entrenchment in scientific debate. Neither master, then, nor above all disciple.

These rules do not trace a method, but very precisely an exodus, a capricious and seemingly irregular trek constrained only by the obligation to avoid speculative places held by force, generally watched over by guard dogs. A walk in the country follows a similar unexpected and jagged trajectory, since there you are attacked, then relentlessly followed, from farm to farm, by ten ferocious hounds, one after another, that you are trying to avoid.

We have at our disposal tools, notions, and efficacy, in great number; we lack, on the other hand, an intellectual sphere free of all relations of dominance. Many truths, very little goodness. A thousand certainties, rare moments of invention. Continuous war, never peace. Only animals savor hierarchy and the unceasing battles that organize it. We lack a simple, democratic intellect for man. Let us define this sphere under the notion of prescription.

Only a peaceful notion will do.

Vengeance produces a seeming justice, the distributive equivalence of an eye for an eye. Everyday language takes one for the other, when, for example, it counsels the victim of an attack to take justice into his own hands: dole it out yourself then. Punishment replaces or buys back the offense that a scale balances: one for another. One does not pronounce the quantum law that would suppose an equality in the order of magnitude, but lex talionis, whose Latin origin (just . . . as) indicates a finer, qualitative, essential distribution: a tooth is not worth an eye.

This vengeful invariance launches a process that no reason could stop because reason itself is equivalent to full and complete reparation, satisfying the offended who demands that the injury be put right and obtains this. The full cause is found, in quantity, in quality, in the entire effect: the rational law of justice and of mechanics. That is enough: injustice would consist of an excess or a lack in the reparation. Which is why it is called reason: not a quantitative equality, but a proportion that is precisely adapted to the plaintiffs and the complaint; one considers the weight placed on both pans, but also the relations of length on the beam of the scale, which in this way renders strict justice.

The principle of reason or, rather, of putting someone in the right [*rendre raison*] (*principium reddendae rationis*) comes from nothing else: nothing, it says, is without reason. This nothing comes from *res*, a word from Roman law that designates the legal case a trial debates and on which it rules: the cause. Before signifying causality, the term *res* bespeaks accusation. One must put right as in a reciprocity, as if reason came in second. Nothing without a reason and a thing without a cause express not so much absurdity or contradiction as a disparity in balance on the scale of justice: to this nothing, to this something, which seem suspended in the air, without support, one must, in compensation, add or subtract a tare that returns the beam—beautiful word—to the horizon, the tare to reason. We do not know how to think something in isolation, hung without attachment or floating without weight: the verb *to think* itself derives from slope and weight, from this compensation. How can we think without compensation, without the rational tare? Thus reason does justice for the thing, thus the cause makes it right.

Here is a principle that must be called equivalence or equity.

That there exists, likewise, something rather than nothing, or this (as such) rather than that—here are two statements that describe two departures from equilibrium, departures that require, in order to combat injustice, a tare to return them to the correct horizontal and planar, position. What to place on the other pan to redeem the harm done to this nothing that did not even achieve existence and to that, otherwise qualified, which remained in virtual or potential worlds? Reason justifies the existence of what is by compensating the potential or nothingness. Measured or weighed by this yardstick, existence, whose troubled name still indicates a departure from equilibrium, equals reason added to nothingness, a rigorous equation. Inversely, does mathematical equality also lead back to the law of justice?

What does one call thinking then? Compensating what is not by means of reason, bringing the rational tare between existence and nothingness or the possible, as if reason constituted the relation of being to nonbeing, or as if it justified what is based on what is not. Thus it touches on quasi-divine creation and supposes a mortal familiarity with nothingness or the possible. This rational thinking, this weight or compensatory proportion, fulfills the ontological lack exactly.

Reason avenges nothingness.

Giving equity to existence, the principle of reason brings ontology under the universal law of rightness. Fulfilling the ontological lack, reason makes it so that all of the knowledge that ensues from it ensues from juridical equilibrium.

Inventor of the principle of sufficient reason, Leibniz calls laws of justice the rules of invariance and stability by which things as well as statements are compensated. Does this reparative reason conserve some trace in science or rationalism of the vengeful eye for an eye?

In medieval or Renaissance astronomy, why call just, in the juridical sense, the long equilibria of the universe or the economy, understood as a positive legislation of the physical world, *justness* or *justice*, appearing through the invariances or stabilities, the circular returns and compensations of cosmic time? The laws of nature, reduced to such harmonies, go back to the principle of sufficient reason. Giving the reason for a phenomenon consists of compensating it, thus rendering it thinkable. Is this a kernel of public prosecution and conviction in the world and thought, or their respective order?

The distributive invariance of vengeance launches a process that nothing, without reason, would be able to stop: thus the long equilibria of the world are counted all along the eternal return. The offended, obtaining reason from the injury, inflicts on he offender an exactly equal harm of equivalent nature, to make of this last a third offended man demanding, in turn, equilibrium or a sufficient reason: the vendetta does not cease, and history conspires and consents to the rhythmic return of constellations as well as to the rules of weighed thought. Everything is in order: the cosmos and time strike, bringing back the hour of compensations.

Here is the immobile motor of our movements, reason in the world and in history, the twin of vengeance, imitating its compensations or reparations, just as the learned who give themselves over to thought inside the classroom walls imitate the hoodlums who fight in the courtyard when the bell rings.

We others, advanced rationalists, illuminated by the most profound laws that reign over the world of atoms, call all of that, sometimes, the balance of terror. The same order always governs the world.

Vengeance and its apparent justice, founding the eternal return, keep the complete memory of exact reason intact, through reversible and cyclical time. They know nothing of duration, that irreversible time that goes in one direction without ever being able to turn back. Forgetting intervenes during the course of duration; where anamnesis neither restores nor compensates exact or intact memory, the whole effect is never equal to complete and total reason; this new time creates a lack in sufficiency, a flaw in or an excess of reason.

In French law, this lack, excess, or flaw is called *prescription*.

It is defined, in civil law, as the legal means of acquiring property through uninterrupted possession and in that case is called acquisitory prescription. Liberating oneself from a charge, for example from a debt, when the creditor does not demand that it be discharged, is called extinctive or liberatory prescription. In criminal law, a time limit is calculated that, once past, precludes any public action being taken against the criminal or the delinquent.

In summary, prescription admits the essential action of time. Usucapion equals right of property, as if the passage of time, in and of itself, effaced the rights of everyone else, in particular those of the possible predecessor. In the same way, when the creditor does not ask for anything and the public ministry attacks no one, time, of itself, suspends or changes action.

Time passes and does not flow in a passive manner; on the contrary, it forgets or effaces acts. It does not return to put right. Linked to the eternal return and to stable invariances, vengeance, astronomical, returns like the constellations or the comets.

It is said that the river Forgetting runs in the Underworld: prescription returns it to the earth, whose sons, seated on the banks of rivers, often lose their memory at the same time as their reason. There is no world more atrocious than the one where nature delivers itself over to the eternal return and pushes forgetting and mercy back into the Underworld. Prescription brings it back or puts it on its feet: real and sweet is the world where the rivers run toward the mouths of forgetting and the ghost of truth is pushed back to the Underworld: *aletheia,* frozen, does not flow.

In physical fact, when the planets return to themselves, wear and tear has gnawed at them a bit, and the red giants of the sky explode at the hour of their supernova. The great invariances drift, the world has lost the eternal return.

In the third position between law and nonlaw, prescription falls by definition into the irreversible domain of history and opposes its annual or thirty-year lapses of time to the invariable and inviolable rules. More than limiting them, it annuls the laws that are in force concerning charges, debts, property, offenses, and crimes. Suddenly, it's as if you no longer owed anything, as if you had never robbed or killed; time, like a baptismal river, makes you innocent. Prescription traces in law the limit of nonlaw, its boundary with history. Prescription, we know, rubs out traces, takes away the remainders, erodes the deeds and the facts, forgets and ends up being silent, in the same way that time cares nothing for the principle of contradiction.

Through its codes and its texts, law is an integral part of the memory of the social computer. It has had a hand in constructing this memory. It fights against the usury of history. This is why its emblem outlines a scale, simultaneously for the symmetry of space, the equivalence of charges, and the regular return of time. This is why, on the side of vengeance, it remains rational. This is why it has always been more or less linked, at its limit or boundary, on the other side, the intemporal side, with natural law, which, in fact, is said to be unprescriptible. On this boundary time exerts no action of itself, and reason, stable throughout this passive time, remains unvarying throughout its passage.

Uneasily, heroically, law stands between two zones, two temptations: one, occupied by natural law, universal and unvarying, unwritten and therefore unprescriptible, intemporal; and the other, invaded by history and the colorfully patterned forgettings of its tatters. Depending on the epoch, it leans, in sum, toward one side or the other, toward maximum law or nonlaw, some would say from rigorous reason to chaos, others would say from an idealized phantom to the complex apprehension of the concrete.

Just as we have put time back on Earth and on its feet by reversing the old map of the Underworld and the globe (given that, taking everything into account, the river Lethe flows like love and its forgettings), we must turn this specter around head to head in order for the single universal and unprescriptible law to become prescription. There is no invariant except on condition that it be thrown into the variable; we no longer conceive of equilibria except in movements.

Reason avenges nothingness, and rational science conserves the traces of this primitive law that one calls natural, without examining this nature that remains foreign to the work of time. For the most positive laws, our acts are immersed in time; but for prescription, they are made and are formed in time, their true primary matter. Duration knots them together, exalts them, unknots them, effaces them. It gives birth to them and makes them vanish. Here nature has come: whatever will be born, yes or no. Nature runs or flows from bifurcation to bifurcation, from turbulent and lively confluents to dead, forgotten branches. It can pass neither for definitively stable nor for madly or irrationally unstable.

Just as it creates our acts, real time creates law, and, if it creates it, it dismantles it just as easily, and that is what the natural is—what keeps being born or risks not being born. Time creates the law, forms it, transforms it, and thus founds it. Jurisprudence, which fluctuates, as is well known, creates law on the side of history, but law recognizes this in recognizing the action of time, through prescription. This is the opening of the law toward its own foundation, that is to say, toward the law that, along with the Ancients, I call natural, that is to say toward physical nature. In making it vary, in annulling it, prescription, though stable, founds it. Natural law, in the most profound sense of the word, is not found on the side where one expected it but on the other, separated from the first by the whole formidable expanse of the sky. Prescription is part of natural law and through it founds law and through it remains unprescritable. The only act that we can neither efface nor annul is the act of annulling or effacing. One does not forget forgetting, in some sense an unforgettable act.

All of that concerns law, but the following concerns morality, politics, and theology: the pardon founds ethics, clemency founds power, holding back or mercy cloaks justice and descends on destiny.

As the term indicates, and as it signified in Roman law, prescription is written at the top, as a preamble or preliminary, as an epigraph to every text. When you write in the morning, once the hour strikes, of theory or literature, of law, science, mathematics or love, know that before the blank page, in its top margin, prescription always already precedes you. By definition, it alone exists before. Written at the top of the page but rubbed out and leaving the page intact, free, virgin, white, innocent. In the third position: inscribed, effaced.

For two millennia at least, everyone remembers but everyone has forgotten that the Samaritans had the worst of roles, that of hateful, implacable, irreconcilable enemies. The parable of the good Samaritan enounces a contradiction: such a man cannot pass for good. Everyone remembers this, everyone has forgotten it: prescription certainly exists and it has succeeded.

Prescription asks for forgetting, but it has already written memory, because it has left its trace. It remembers being written but prescribes forgetting. It in no way equals conservation, nor does it identify itself with dead loss; it invents anew, as in a third place, memory-forgetting, the memory kept sheltered but at the same time effaced, intellectually unvarying in the black box of history, but passionately, essentially, historically, wisely lost: a new invariant through variations, stability through instabilities, another foundation of the law stronger than the dreary eternal return, immobile like a sack of lead or ringing like a bell.

In order not to write any longer except in the beauty or love of wisdom, we will no longer write philosophy except by prescription.

When it is possible to read without scandal a narrative where the most abominable man now behaves like the best, the Messiah will come. But he has already come, because he wrote this text of which I am not the author.

Me. Night

The author? Who is he, who am I?

Admirably named, the subject, modest or terrified, hides, jumps behind or beneath the succession of clothing, is thrown beneath the capes and coats, subjected to them, unlocatable like Harlequin, whose striptease always and everywhere showed the same thing, with a few variations more or less, of the colorful pattern, whether it be a question of suit, of skin, of sex, or of blood, ultimately of soul—*my soul of a thousand voices that the god that I honor placed in the center of everything like a sonorous echo*—whose juxtaposed facets, like those of a crystal or a fly's eye, reflect, though intimate, the rustling multiplicity of external events, as if the number of them corresponded to the number of interior walls that reflect them. Can one seek more as well? From the comparative— the interior—to the superlative—the intimate? Is there something more intimate still? Does what lies below always resemble what one can see on the surface?

Lacking the subject, I can name the adjective. If the first throws itself below, that is if others don't throw it there, the second is thrown aside. For the question, "Who am I?" either I substitute the question, "Who is he?" or modesty requires that I always seek to respond beside the point. That is, with some adjectives.

Who am I? It is said that I am genteel, an esteemed adjective in my country where one likes the old words of the nobility—genteel, thus attentive, supple and adapted, courteous. I quickly divine positive qualities in the other, and at that moment I smile, but, naive, do not know how to suspect vices. Rapidly, the adjectives overabound. Confident, I willingly enjoy the encounter, by cheerfully giving contingency its chance. Timid or fearful, it seems, I am not wary, can one say courageous, then? My initial esteem for the other, who encourages it and often fortifies it, makes me always place the level above me, at first I only find better than myself: generous? Maybe, but then suddenly I discover that I am throwing myself under, as a result, I am a bit subject; at least subjugated. I define myself through contacts, neighborhoods, encounters, and relations: yes, in communication, I construct myself by throwing myself immediately under my opposite. Finally subject?

But I become suddenly aware of it: wasn't the word *subject* itself an adjective that belatedly became a noun? First dependent, submitted, compelled, exposed, indeed obliged, just as I can say to whomever I am speaking: thank you, I am much obliged to you . . . before taking myself for the point of departure of a logical and grammatical statement where this individual being becomes a person and the basis for acts and knowledge. An adjective so well cast aside that it bespoke the docile and the obedient and that, suddenly, took the principal place and, in nominalizing itself, expelled the other adjectives outside the center where, in philosophy, its majesty took the throne? Must one recognize, in the subject, a subject that could unduly have taken the central place, a comic king like Harlequin, Emperor of the Moon, or a tragic king, tortured, traversed by arrows in the center?

What am I then, when, thus, I throw myself under? Admiring, even enthusiastic, for whoever is revealed to be inventive and good, respectful of whoever works, surprised by the generous person, violently disobedient to whoever commands or thunders or pronounces the law, sweetly ironic before the peacock, moved by the beauty of the body or of talent, frigid before the grandeur of the establishment, quickly breaking off with the vain, I present my homages to chambermaids—by birth, I belong to the family of the humble, and rarely bow down before the highest rank; thus, depending on the person and the entourage, I am loquacious, taciturn, talkative, warm, reserved, absent, or totally given over to the other. Who then have you met, you who like me or hate me, to whom I become hostile or indifferent? A jovial or modest man, savage, distracted, on the contrary, concentrated . . .

All the same, all that is true. Tell me, I beg you, what is meant by a lie? The relation produces the person; I do not fully believe in masks. Tucked away, thrown alive under the moving "we" of intersubjectivity, the self, as one says, does what it can: it adapts, subject to the bonds of communication. Half-breed, quadroon, hermaphrodite, ambidextrous, tattooed, living under a thousand layers of patchwork coats, I can get rid of them without a lot of trouble—that does not change much. Do not accuse the profiles that others sketch in me of being masks.

The servant of a thousand masters, Harlequin dresses in his subjects-spectators, because he remains in the public arena and is part of it, this is why he remains a comedy emperor, whereas Solomon, external and far away, encumbered by his solar madness, becomes a true tragedy king. In flames, the tragic, alone, forges the unity of the person at the same time as those of action, place, and time—the subject of knowledge itself, at least in the West, is founded on the tragic—the comic leaves them to their multiplicity. Subject to his subjects, the Emperor of the Moon wears their colors and their jerseys. Irresistibly, I diagnose the essential theater of the mentally ill in the solar tragedian: the comedian, normal, is a dime a dozen.

Who am I then, once again? Solitary and social, timid and courageous, humble and free, burning, touchy, animal of flight and love, I never wear powder or foundation, nor painted cardboard on my face, nor place a title beneath my signature and on my visiting card. I feel the clothing under my skin like a naked man who is covered. I am numerous enough to have never had the need to lie.

In reality, I am thus all those that I am in and through the successive or juxtaposed relations in which I find myself involved, productive of me, adjectivized subject, subjected to the collective we, and free from myself. May the reader pardon me: I only speak of myself (of myself, truly?) in order to seek as faithfully as possible what the reader is about. Thus the self is a mixed body: studded, spotted, zebrine, tigroid, shimmering, spotted like an ocelot, whose life must be its business. Here Harlequin's coat returns, sewn from adjectives, I mean to say from terms placed side by side.

Thus the unfortunate awakens in me the old Christian who always sleeps with one eye open and who gives birth to a new Christian, on a heap of straw; the powerful brings back the ancient Cathar, always present despite the fact that an authentic Holocaust eradicated the whole sect—I no longer have any forefathers; someone dogmatic and opinionated brings out the slumbering mocker, and the fool brings out the inextinguishable laugh of the gods, the violent man arouses the pacifist, and beauty brings them all to their knees.

Am I then a backdrop by relation, a fleeting profile effaced before a deceptive and lying horizon? No, I am the sum of these adjectives, newly nominalized (one rightly says the "nouveaux riches"), the ichnography of these silhouettes, a nervous and fluctuating summation, plunged in noise and furor, in the midst of the squawking, of the hurly-burly of parasites who gravitate around this self, an exile bathed in the gift of tears, thorax drowned in a lake of tears, a total liquid solitude, in an unstable state, a solution without exclusion in which the flux of abandon suddenly crosses the variable space of courage, in which the yellow coating of awakening is frayed and thrown into the black volume of forgetting, in which some sudden jets of pride spurt momentarily from a basin of oily humility . . . Yes, the adjectives are immersed of themselves in each other and play unceasingly at being the subject: a melee in which each goes by turn and sometimes all go at once to the center, but where they occupy all the places and all the directions of space, all senses.

What I am, from this point on, is expressed without difficulty: a mixture, a good- or bad-tempered melee, a temperament, to be precise. The word saying the thing itself, I am, by consequence, made of time, of the time derived from temperature or from temperance. Like time, the mixture is contradictory: from yesterday to tomorrow, all can be reversed; or, in the same place, at the same time, everything is combined.

Mixture and time are contradictory, just as is my cloudy, variable, wavy, nuanced, Aquitanian soul. My soul, mixture, and time can be named neither by nouns, too stable, nor by adjectives, too juxtaposed, but are most accurately described by all the prepositions together: *before* and *after* construct their viscous fluidity; *with* and *without*, the hesitating divisions; *over* and *under*, the false and true subject; *for* and *against*, the violent passions; *behind* and *before*, the cowardly hypocrisies and courageous loyalties; *in* and *outside of*, the corporeal and theoretical, social and professional claustrophobias; *between* and *beyond*, the metaphysical vocation of the archangel-messenger; *from* and *via* and *toward*, my furor to travel . . . a fine topology that best expresses the places and neighborhoods, the ruptures and continuities, the accumulations and scarcities, the positions and sites, the flux and evolutions, the liquidity of solvents and solutions.

No, I am not a problem; literally, I am a solution. And I would tolerate writing titles on my visiting card on condition that the title comprise the diverse relations of the substances dissolved in it, their density in the alloy. Who am I? A fusion of alloys, more coalescent than coalesced.

Of an Aquitanian disposition, thus, tempered like the climate of my native landscape, melancholically cheerful, enthusiastic and desperate, with soft nuances, in changing doses and with mobile titles, depending on the moment and whether I fall in with the right or wrong sort of people, each part or suspension capable of suddenly finding itself raised, awakened, or spotlighted beneath the crossbeam of circumstances or intersections, due to the sudden demand of a powerful and punctual relation.

A sort of pseudopod advances. It stretches. It will retract. Perhaps it will never reappear. Or will become the axon. What will I invent today beneath the force of some dove's foot? What new property will emerge from this new mixture? What fresh Aphrodite will be born, shimmering, from this unexpected churning?

Legion, I am octaroon. Thus I carry in myself, in the most intimate part of me (I was going to say beneath me) the composite rags of the fabrics that clothe my real and virtual entourage, the rags and tatters in which a thousand mimes are badly juxtaposed, my time has sewn them, then melted them together, tattered rags, certainly, but rags become my very flesh, my mixed liquid blood: Quebecois from the island of Coudres in the middle of the Saint Lawrence, African from the banks of the Niger, Chinese from the Yangtze, Brazilian from Belém on the lip of the Amazon, the locative adjectives in turn abound, my blood runs beneath the banks of the Garonne, of the Mackenzie and the Yukon, my flesh emerges from the lillies of the Garonne, of the Amur, of the Ganges and the Nile, I descend from the Garonne, from the Huang, from the Elbe and from the Mississippi, from the Pactolus and the Jordan, sailor of the Sea at the confluence of the rivers of the Earth, my visiting card resembles my visits, the map of geography. Quadroon, I am legion, I am not the devil, I am the world map and all the world at the same time.

And everybody, I think, is a mixture like me, blood diluted for a thousand reasons and in a thousand quarters, flowing from all the rivers at once, except, maybe those who read and believed the books that explain the principle of identity, whose abridged version allows one to reign. World, I am legion; no, it is not an illness.

The Africans never believed that I was a *toubab* or European, the Chinese thought I was from some national minority, everywhere an immigrant rather than an émigré, an American Indian even asked me, during a powwow, to which tribe I belonged. I believe, in my very depths, that belonging causes the evil in the world, by reason of exclusion. Half-breed, I take care of belonging through the intersection of one thousand memberships.

Peasant, yes, I learned to labor; spice vendor, certainly, I sold oil and salt; sailor, assuredly; hunter of stones and mason, did I do anything else in the course of my life? Vagrant, maybe, monk, certainly; I recently became a novice mountain climber; passionately in search of saintliness; writer, yes, I hope; philosopher, I cry with emotion and hope at the idea that I could become one . . . Yes, all, I include them all.

What am I not? Bull, snake, lynx, dog, wolf, gull? I am and I comprise the whole Ark. From the fluid flood and the dissolved alliance. What animal would not serve me as a totem? A fox? No, I live like an animal without a species. With no genus, of mixed blood, without membership: free, free in the iridescent space of mixtures, a beast of temperance and of temperament, a being of time.

Who am I, liquid, among the hidden tears? Who am I, topological and temporal? When, finally, silence and night insulate solitude, once language, which holds the seat of the others in me, is quiet—how to muzzle the beak of this incurable chatterer?—then voices are raised, the fundamental musical tonality that has accompanied me since remotest childhood, continues without a break, a continuous tearing, armor or armature that carries me, and whose tessitura indicates my own modality, pure sounds deprived of meaning, I am, I hear the flute and the cello, the lullaby and the canon, the mandora and the tuba, hurdy-gurdy and rebec, dawn serenade and ballet, cavatina and rigadoon, soprano, singing bass, in me I carry the great organs, my delights and loves: great bell, organ stop, and larigot. But, again, these pieces or instruments are combined, sometimes harmonized, often quarrelsome, always plaintive, hurly-burly, charivari, atonal acouphenics from which, on rare occasions, the streaming Aphrodites of musical inspiration—or a pure cry of pain—emerge.

At the bottom of the bottom lies and moves music, a united and turbulent flux and river, the portage and reach of time, at the bottom of the bottom of the bottom the background noise fluctuates.

There I throw myself into the world of things that throw themselves into me.

Me: brute quarreling. Me: long note. Me: pronoun, when language, finally, gets into the melee, to forget (the only true lie) the combinations and efface the multiplicity of pieces. Me: third person, each, the others, all, that, the world, and the impersonal *it* of temporal intemperate weather: it rains, it cries, it is windy . . . and it complains; it thunders, shouts . . . music, noise; suddenly, it must, and here I am, ethical, gathered together, up, at work, since dawn.

Classical philosophy advises passing from modes and attributes, which are circumstantial, to substance; from adjectives, flighty and inconstant, to the stable and fixed noun: but the word *subject,* as I said, was an adjective before transforming itself into a noun. Cheat! One would say that flightiness, after having lived, settled down.

When you hear or compose variations on a given theme, don't you sometimes ask yourself if the theme itself doesn't develop like one variation among others? Simpler, doubtless, purer, shorter, certainly, but why separate it from them? There is as much distance between the variations as between them and the theme, which nothing prevents me from calling a variation on one of the variations. Why prejudge it as more stable and more centered than they? Yes, the theme is nothing but one of the variations.

Thus the king himself is a subject, a man among so many others, two feet, ten fingers, in the best cases, with his supports on the same earth as mine. The proof is that, ever since the guillotine welcomed him, all his former subjects, with a few rare and wise exceptions, dream of taking his place or of arranging it to welcome the temporary king, who never ceases to be a subject, more subject even than the first, in the political sense, because the number of assassination attempts directed against him are far above the number of those plotted against just anyone. He is thrown below: he must know that he owes his place as king to the fact that he is the most subjected of subjects.

Nominalized adjective, theme-variation, citizen-king; likewise the central sun is nothing but a marginal star, a yellowish and mediocre dwarf, without true grandeur, in the immense concert of supergiants, red like Betelgeuse or blue like Rigel. If King Solomon returned among us, would he say, Nothing new under the galaxy of Cygnus? It has been a long time since the astrophysical revolution taught us to no longer center the sky or the universe. It is even said that the big bang's point of origin would have had no site or time.

Thus the center is nothing but a centon, a numerous ensemble of composite pieces. You ask the Emperor of the Moon to get undressed to show what he is hiding: well, he is not concealing anything. Everything is truly always and everywhere as it is here, give or take a few degrees of magnitude and perfection, I mean to say that everything is a Harlequin's coat, even substance, even the theme, even the subject, even the self, even the king, even the sun, even nouns. Singularity is scattered, unity multiplies.

Even God? Isn't he one of the secrets that I unveil: singular and triple, multiple, adjective and noun, divine and divinity, king and subject, supergiant in his central glory and dwarf lost in a manger at the periphery, universal and singular, creative law, tragic incarnation ready to die, the third person propagated everywhere?

Absurd, impossible, inadmissible: I did not dare to say it; no, I have never had the courage to expose what I believe.

But first of all: I do not know if I believe, I know nothing of what it is to believe, I do not know what thought, what act, or what feeling accompanies belief or faith. I know, somewhat, what it is to know, I know what I know, when I know it, what I do to know it, I know ignorance and doubt, research and questioning, I know knowledge, its happiness and its objects, its multiple paths, its enthusiastic quest and its deserts, its profound humility, its rare and necessary forgetting of dominating reason. And I recognize what I feel, modestly arranged forever in a black box. Would the mixture of an uncertain knowledge and a certain abandoned pathos left behind be what one would call belief? I do not know. Or I know that I am indifferent to it. What does it matter to me to learn whence comes what I will dare to say: I am old enough, that is to say, strong enough, to have the courage.

I do not know if I believe in God. I know that often I cannot believe in God: I am an atheist three-fourths of the time. Yet, through intermittent flashes, I know that the divine is there, present, in my neighborhood, and that it reigns through the universe. Here, *reign* does not refer in any way to a king, but to that means of construction that a tiler indicates when he says that a hexagonal and red floor tile reigns in, is spread throughout, all the rooms of the same house. Everywhere in the universe, the divine is the fabric, the others say the law, I prefer to describe its matter or flesh, of which I am certain, not now, but sometimes, rarely, in an ecstatic manner. And when the long eclipse follows the brief, intuitive flash, I am certain that God is not: it's an outdated and unnecessary hypothesis. Maybe, then, he abandons me, doubtless he damns me, in abandoning my intelligence to this misery. Did God abandon all of us ever since that recent day when we abandoned him?

I do not believe, I believe; that cannot be decided, but ensues. Mystic miscreant, my rare assurances are immersed in dreary incredulity. Now during the moments when I believe, I believe in a single God, a continuous wall of the universe, bedrock, foundation, and pinnacle, inevitable presence, a constant proximity and meaning . . . but I cannot, for long, leave the woods uninhabited by hamadryads, the sea without Sirens, and the wars of nations without their hideous sacred, the towns without temples of difference, and their dwellings without the spirits of their forebearers: the air is peopled with passing archangels, with innumerable messengers; yes, here I am truly pagan, I admit it, polytheistic, a peasant son of a peasant, a sailor son of a mariner, I have sometimes seen the gods flee from an island that I was approaching, or appear in glory, I have heard them cackle, cruel, abominable, incarnated as all powers, I have often heard legions of demons released in the thundering of canons, yes, I was floored by the devil himself—Who did not perceive his monstrous body outlined, real, behind the clouds of the atomic blast?—but I have also seen a light goddess pass among smiles; on my philosopher's word, I have seen them, I have witnessed it.

I believe, sometimes, in the God of my father, an atheist suddenly converted amid the shells on the battlefield of Verdun; I believe, often, in the gods of my oldest forebearers; I know that, besides me, they fill space, that they constitute the world; especially, that they solder society.

Since Nagasaki, I am seduced, even more, by my Cathar ascendance; a crowd of gods reduced to two, of which one, that of evil, remains the undisputed master of all that men call the power and the glory, history, while the one of goodness hides and disappears in the straw in a manger, so removed, common, effaced, that he remains inaccessible. All for the first, nothing for the second, who is disfigured, beaten, improbable.

I believe, I believe especially, I believe essentially that the world is God, that nature is God, white waterfall and laugh of the seas, that the variable sky is God Himself: I have navigated in God, flown in the midst of God, received his true light on my back in the corridors of ice high up on the mountains, at dawn; I have even composed, sometimes, under his breath, while naively tracing my path of humility on the divine page, and because of this vocation, I have never ceased to survive through him, with him and in him . . . but, above all, you are God, you whom I love and you who hate me, you who pass by and whom I will never know, you who have excluded me, you from whose lips I received springtime flowers, you finally who make up the noise, the hurly-burly of my carnal and categorial life . . .

. . . but what is more I am sure, absolutely certain beyond all hope, that there exists a hole, a bizarre flaw in this massive and dense pantheism, a strange exception, source of all pain, that I and *I alone,* in this divine concert traversed by quarreling, am not God; yet this fault line of nothingness is not God; a new, very pointed, meaning of the old word *atheist.* Here, no God. Here, only, God is absent. My portion of destiny is this site of atheism.

Everything is God except the one who writes him, who lets fall His pen amid tears.

The one. The center. The sun. The theme. Substance. God. The proper name: Solomon, Harlequin, the author of this book.

The manifold. The composite periphery. Stars of every magnitude. Variations. Attributes, the ragged coat. Multiple adjectives: genteel, courteous, talkative, taciturn. . . Further ahead: the dissolved mixture, music, time, the grainy noise made by mills, souls, and the sea.

The manifold and unity are in reality, like limit singularities in a variation. Here is the simple image. Take a mosaic: it juxtaposes millions of elements in various forms and various colors, whose limits outline a sort of network. This is the manifold: world map, Harlequin's coat, a centon of various texts.

Let a picture painted in oil on canvas represent the same scene as the mosaic: the network disappears, the vicinities dissolve, the elements, erased, give way to a continuous slope of forms and mixed colors. In *La Belle Noiseuse,* an unknown masterpiece by a nameless painter, a superb foot emerges from a chaos of tonalities.

In the corresponding geometric graph, immersed in a homogeneous and isotropic space, curves are displayed according to laws and get their bearings thanks to straight lines (both vertical and horizontal), points have no parts, neither lines nor planes have any depth: here the reign of one succeeds that of the manifold in the mosaic, that of the mixture of liquid colors on the canvas.

We can, on the one hand, take the mosaic from the painting, by having it cut up, then by making a puzzle or a game of patience of it based either on its traits or section by section. The mixture thus tends toward the manifold, *partes extra partes.* The discontinuous emerges from continuity, like whole numbers on the line of real numbers. The elements dissolved in the mixture are well or badly separated. The mosaic shows the grains. In the most extreme case you could say that, seemingly, if you could see *La Belle Noiseuse* from infinitely close up, you would find this granular arrangement.

One can imagine, conversely, a mixture diluted to the point that the colors would vanish to allow homogeneity to appear. A drop of honey, a cloud of milk, a pint of blood in the Mediterranean would not be able to disturb this uniformly wine-colored sea. So the complicated volutes are simplified to the extreme, every detail is annulled and objects are vitrified: approximation makes room for rigor, mixture tends infinitely toward purity and painting toward geometry.

In the final analysis, the manifold and the singular become limit singularities of mixture. Mixture never ceases, remains, surrounds and bathes us, doubtless it must be called reality, which we conceive with the help of two opposed singularities: reality's limit on the side of the singular, and its other limit on the faces of the manifold—Harlequin dressed in his coat, Solomon and his sun.

Monism and pluralism are limit philosophies abstractly con-structed against a real background of mixture. The first geometrizes it, whereas the second proposes a mosaic, a cutout in the form of a puzzle, an image on a television screen.

How can we speak of mixture? By means, once again, of prepo-sitions. If we had to describe *La Belle Noiseuse* or Harlequin's coat, we would have to draw unceasingly from the list or rubric of prepo-sitions: such a color or form is found in or outside, before or between, beside and against, over or under, according to or until this one or that one: topology has returned.

Now there exists a topology of geometry's first graph, one of the mosaic, finally another one of painting. Thus, the rigorous descrip-tion that topology proposes or the one that uses prepositions is good for all three schemas. Which is what I wanted to show.

Now, to pass from mixture to the manifold and from the mani-fold to unity, we traverse a space or a time that vibrates and trem-bles like the curtain of flames illuminating the ramp of the theater where Harlequin undressed. Sometimes we perceive the singular, soon we distinguish the manifold or swim in the melee.

But I can still describe, in the same way, the dance of fire that illuminates us, through continuous, torn up, short, long, faraway, neighboring sparks, over and under, outside and in, before, behind, after, in front of, beyond and between . . .

Which is what I wanted to show.

Fire. I imagine a pyramid, a prism that is absolutely transparent. When the white light of the day, itself invisible, but capable of mak-ing everything visible, is cast on a face of this candid prism, it comes out on the other side in a rainbow of dissolved and distinct colors: not a single one is missing. Stellar spectrum, Harlequin's coat.

Who am I? No one, strictly speaking. Nil. So pale and gaunt that I lose my existence. Pallid and wan specter, ready to dissolve in the air. Nothing, strictly speaking. White, invisible, candid, and trans-parent. Zero. A pure solid entirely given over to light, no matter where light comes from, high and low, brilliant, subdued, estab-lished or irregular. Not a single portion of being, nothing but noth-ingness.

Therefore, everything. The white light on the translucent pyramid explodes according to the more than multicolored spectrum of panchromaticism. Nothing, therefore everything. Nil, therefore possible. No one, therefore everyone. White, therefore all values. Transparent, therefore welcoming. Invisible, therefore productive. Nonexistent, therefore indefinitely fit for the universe. Once again here is the law.

Universally, then, because man is nothing, he can: infinite capacity.

I am no one and am worth nothing—capable, then, of learning everything and of inventing everything, body, soul, understanding, and wisdom. Since God and man are dead, reduced to pure nothingness, their creative power is resurrected.

That is why I was able to write this book, and why I had to: because apprenticeship, of which you see the foundation, is the white essence of the hominid.

You. Day

Envoi. My friend Hergé did not want a last name, I suppose, since he signed with only the initials of his two first names, Rémi and Georges.[1] Such an acronym shows and hides that he had hardly begun to be or exist, like a child. Modesty detaches the essential and reserves it. As for Tintin, he has no name, not even a nickname, just an onomatopoeia. We evoke these two shadows, we do not call to them.

Who then, trait by trait, was the one who thrilled our childhood?

Georges was white: luminous, diaphanous, dazzling, but calm. An enthusiast or inventor of the clear line, at work, he inhabited a house of light colors and a limpid, pure body. I remember him as a transparency, his intelligence levitated; I already knew when we spoke together that I was dealing with an angel. Tintin resembles him but especially Blessed Lightning. In the high-altitude areas of Tibet all the keys of the secret are discovered: white snow, the monk in ecstasy, the lost friend, and the abominable one who turns

1. In French the initials *R G* sound like "Hergé" since the *H* is unaspirated. Belgian artist Georges Rémi (aka Hergé) wrote the Tintin comic books.— TRANS.

out to be good.[2] No more mean people sacrificed or punished, the atrocious world of victories and defeats finally flattened, a great conversion, exactly the opposite of the one recommended to him. The clear line unveils all these incandescences.

Thus Georges, or Hergé, who signed his name in white, loved a colorist.

Thirty rays converge toward the hub, says a Chinese proverb, but the small void right in the middle confers strength, coherence, and function on the wheel. More than twenty books radiate like a dawn from this life, but how to name the crystalline, transparent and white light that gave birth—through what prism?—to these images in which millions of children and adults have recognized themselves for so long?

How can a name for it be found? Genius? Yes, of the notable and truly famous people that I have encountered in my life, I think I can say that Georges stands out as the only true genius. Try to cite a single work read continuously for more than half a century by several generations, each rereading it as the following generation discovers it. Genius is not only defined by this growing recognition, but especially by the secret relation that it maintains with the two positive manifestations of life: the comic and childhood. The very young nieces and the white-haired uncle laugh together at Molière and Aristophanes, whom no one surpasses in force and vigor. The high moments of culture begin with these great bursts of youthful gaiety: creativity laughs.

In the snows of the Himalayas, Hergé loses the last negative values, so that his work says an immense Yes, solitary and rare in a century that loved, in its art and in its actions, destruction and ruins, and that delights in sterility. What does this naive, native, confiding, living, vital, laughing, and new Yes, transparent, ingenuous, announce for us, children up to the age of seventy-seven, before our works that are yet to be completed?

The white domino equals all the colors, virtually: depending on whether one puts it here or there, it is one, two, or three. It owes

2. Reference to *Tintin in Tibet*, where, in searching for his lost friend Chang, Tintin discovers that the greatly feared abominable snowman may actually "have a human soul." Blessed Lightning is a monk.—TRANS.

this performance to its whiteness: the zero sum and union of all colors, it contains them and effaces them, everything and nothing. White light is broken down into the spectrum of the rainbow and absorbs it, just as the tail of the peacock folds back after it spreads. If you want to become everything, accept being nothing. Yes. The transparent void. This supreme abstraction, this detachment equivalent to polyvalence. Whitened, you will understand all and here you are, at leisure, fish, plant, flower, archangel, or luminary.

Hergé, signing with the initials of his first names, without a name, hardly existing, draws, first in black and white, a quasi-anonymous character, designated by an onomatopoeia, round like the moon, with his head barely outlined, knowing all and capable of everything, capable of everything that is possible, and including around him the fish Haddock, the flora Castafiore, Calculus, and Jolyon Wagg . . . [3] The white domino produces and includes the series of all the dominoes. The creative center, the head of Tintin, or the genius of Georges, shine, incandescent, like the snow or the glaciers of Tibet. Thirty rays, the whole world, Asia, America, the islands of the Pacific rim, the Incas, Indians and Congolese, converge toward the hub where the empty and transparent circle of the middle, the candid center, head of Tintin, angelic soul of Georges, air beneath the feet of Blessed Lightning, ice floe, childhood, all that says Yes alone gives cohesion and plenitude, existence and perfection to the whole wheel.

The vital circumstances, encounters, waits, voyages, hits and misses, work, labor above all, crushing work, massive and dense, invading the days and the hours, occupying the heights, abandoning the body and the soul to the evil of time, all the details of a life given over to work, converge in the center, toward a man, my friend, of whom I publicly testify that, transfigured by it, his face, white, radiated like the sun. How to draw his portrait, in the middle of the rose window, when the light coming from him produced all the drawings, all the portraits exploding on the perimeter of the

---

3. Characters or elements in the Tintin books: Captain Haddock (Tintin's best friend and fellow detective), Bianca de Castafiore (the opera singer); Professor Calculus [Tournesol, literally sunflower], who is kidnapped for his invention, and the tedious insurance salesman Jolyon Wagg [Seraphim Lampion], both appear in *The Calculus Affair*.—TRANS.

stained-glass window, multiple vignettes that have fascinated us since our bitter childhood?

And that fascinate us because the white spot, the inoffensive and almost inexpressive, childlike, indeterminate head of Tintin burns through the page or pierces the casement of one of those windows through which, in fairs and festivals, the one who wants his photographic portrait taken as a hero, star or king, can slide his face or his bust and reappear, on the other side, in a stage set of virgin forest, of a palace or an opera. But it can happen that the muffle of a bull will cover his neck and his shoulders and he will run, staggering, through the props. . . [4]

Each reader thrusts his own body into the straits left by this white absence and says to himself in evoking it: I am Tintin. The adventurer, in turn, whatever he is called, identifies for the same reason and participates as a thousand diverse individuals—from every class, ethnicity, culture, latitude—in the characters of this encyclopedia made up of ellipses and parabolas that make Hergé into the Jules Verne of the first human sciences.

Climbing up from this restless and sweet crowd toward its animator or its creator, one reaches the clear and calm, almost absent light from which a series of transparencies in turn produces a return to depths.

Who has traversed Shanghai, Tibet, Scotland, or the Near East without saying to himself: I recognize this landscape that strangely resembles what I saw in my childhood through the eyes of Chang or the son of the emir? How is it that, fenced in by the war in a loop of the Garonne, I had already traveled so much, learned so many things about men? Things are reversed by magic: the world mimicks the memorable panels, the models reflect the image, life has begun to follow the spells of art. I even know some who would not deign to look at the flowers in the field if they had not first seen poppies in a Renoir: no Île-de-France before Corot. This banal experience, which says a lot about experience, has its origin in the author himself who obeys this bizarre law that inverses the order and the unfolding of things: he submits to it and masters it.

4. Reference to a scene in *The Seven Crystal Balls*, in which Captain Haddock stumbles backstage; while he is crashing around, a mask of a bull's head falls over his own.—TRANS.

The man of work enters body and soul, with blood, joy, and tears, into his work, which begins to produce of its own accord life as it is and the world as it is revealed and thus, in particular, that man who one day set his hand to work. An enchanted circle in which the man and the work feed on each other, the man and the work, a spiral that ends only at the hour of death. We will never know if the panel becomes white because the illustrator dies or if he dies because Tintin, this time, will not emerge from it; a circle of profusion that gives birth to all these stories without borders from Moulinsart,[5] as if from a cornucopia, proof that a lot of people and things are hidden there, beneath the armor and in the outbuildings. Watch out for the one who comes out of there or who leaves a trace: here lies the treasure. Diamonds, rubies, necklaces whose value explodes for a long time on the open trajectory of this invading helix up to the stars but that turns in on itself to feed on the antipodes in the castle, in the fetish, in the cave, in the statue, in the very body of the author, thus produced and producer.

Georges radiated with the white light of a diamond in this treasure. He always looked as if he were emerging from his castle, which haunted him or that he inhabited. The circle rises from I know not where and climbs like an opulent spiral that goes to the extremities of the world and enchants it but that always returns to the vertical of itself: Rameau counts the measures that are born naturally from music itself, whose measures produce the music of Rameau and finally Rameau himself who composes the measures. Georges never ceased entering or leaving that mill.

Thus the portrait of the man is reduced to the eye of the work, just as one says the eye of the cyclone, a calm and sun-filled space, site of the treasure where Georges shone, tranquil and diaphanous.

In those happy hours when he waited for us on the steps of his house, his arms open, his eyes and face illuminated by a smile and by goodness, I never passed along the road to Dieweg without my emotions going beyond gratitude toward the one who had delighted my childhood. Through my tears, I divined the enchanter.

5. Moulinsart is the house where Tintin lives with Captain Haddock.— TRANS.

Bombings, deportations, wars, and mass crimes crushed our childhood, in desperation and sorrow, in shame for our fellow men, except for the singular enchantment that China and the Amazon gave us, shining behind the clear line, and the shattering forgiveness of the abominable monster derided by all and who becomes, seen up close, merciful and good, a conversion in the middle of the immaculate desert. The only lights in the heart of darkness. What good is living if no one ever enchants the world? How and where to live if there is no enchanted place in the middle of these destructions? What if we had survived, in those times and those unlivable places, only thanks to such utopias? Still the eye of the cyclone, the only space where a skiff risks nothing, white silence in the midst of cries.

Between paradise and the dreary landscape, between the bitter valley and the kingdom, the Messiah and the man in the street, difference, infinitesimal, shines like a small tear.

Enchanted things and bodies seem to be immersed in limpid water beneath which they glitter like diamonds or pearls: transfigured by a gloss, an Orient, or a dawn of whose natural source we know nothing; their nimbus dazzles us and protects them.

To make them radiate thus, we content ourselves most often with immersing them in the transparency of language or in the brilliance of style and we sometimes succeed: we see them shine behind clear words or stiffen or settle beneath their rigor when they do not shrivel up beneath the ugliness or the dryness of terms. "The trees and the plants," the fabulist Fontaine would say, "have become speaking creatures in my work, who would not take this for an enchantment?" Here the sunflower and the chaste flower, plants, but also the haddock, a fish, converse with a dog, an animal who usually barks. To perfect the miracle, one can by turn immerse words and languages in the spell of a song *[chant]*, whence comes the word *enchantment.*

Things are immersed in speech and speech plunges into music: a double transfiguration of the world by the poetic work; the entrance of Wagner, going up and down scales in space or the staircase at Moulinsart.[6]

6. Igor Wagner, accompanist to Bianca Castafiore in *The Castafiore Emerald,* who leaves a recording of himself practicing his scales while he slips out.— TRANS.

The illustrator, with his broken ear, does not understand it in this way. For him, enchantment does without song: the ridiculous soprano atrociously executes the aria of the jewels and loses hers, which were believed stolen, whereas they shine calmly in the nest of the panel.[7]

The comic strip opens an original path, different from that of language, of rhythm or of sound, and allows beings and things to radiate from their own forms and in their singular waters: the mute poetry of the clear line. Vignettes replace rhymes and cadenced feet in this classic fabulist with one hundred diverse acts, whose stage is the universe. Here I have found the name of the one who did not want one; note that the fountain *[la fontaine]* reflects the image of shining and tranquil water.

Formerly, portraitists surrounded the heads of saints, martyrs, virgins, or archangels with an aureole whose light marked their transfiguration. Laugh rather at those who laugh at them: most cultures, modern or ancient, have a particular word to designate the glory with which certain bodies sometimes shimmer, in an explosion of energy or love, goodness, ecstasy, and fervent attentiveness. With this sign, one recognizes that someone is thinking: the idea escapes or emanates from his body in a golden glow.

Social glory does nothing but poorly imitate this real aureole that emerges from the face. The great painters, gifted with a keen eye, see it. Or, rather, when they reproduce the things of the world just as they are at the moment their creator's hands give birth to them—infant, initial, with a first name only, beginning—they project, in their painted work, their divine experience and attentiveness.

I no longer know what to choose: does the aureole describe the light that emanates from the model or from the illustrator, or rather does it fix the source of light that illuminates both, or finally, should one see it as the eye that truly sees?

In order to finish the book that bespeaks and describes the circumstances of the life of the third-instructed, as a wheel with

7. Aria sung by soprano Bianca Castafiore in various books, which also references the "Air de bijoux" in Gournod's opera *Faust.*—TRANS.

spokes around its hub, I intended to trace the portrait of my friend, one of the profiles of this life. Having only a first name, here he is: a void in the middle of this radiating circle, a white brilliance, the glow of dawn, a clear aureole, the eye of the painter and of the cyclone, sparkling and calm, just as I knew him, as I loved him, modest, restrained.

The Third Person: Fire

When a man swims across a large river or an arm of the sea (just as in reading or in writing a reader or an author traverses a book and finishes it), at a given moment he crosses an axis, a middle, equidistant from the two banks. Once he's reached it, is continuing straight ahead equivalent to turning around? Before this point, just before this moment, the champion has not yet left his country of origin, whereas after, the exile to which he is destined already submerges him.

A moving thread, slim and fine like a crest, this threshold determines the voyage and every apprenticeship, a rare place that is barely noticed, so abstract that it could be called nonexistent, and yet so pregnant and so concrete that it extends its nature and something like its color across the entire trajectory that consists of crossing it. The breadth of the river or of the training—of the book, and, in its middle *[milieu]*, of the world—feel the effects of it, as if they reproduced this thread writ large.

The limit of a frontier designates, on this side of it, familiar lands, acts as a third party in a division, but a voyage pulls and drags this third place throughout the whole space that is thus divided. Before the frontier, less at home already than usual, the novice swims or is displaced toward the strange; once past it, having almost arrived elsewhere, he is always coming from home: half nervous, at first, and filled with hope; already nostalgic, after, and soon half-regretful. How then can a singular place pass for rare and, nevertheless, be disseminated everywhere, on the ground and in the soul, remain abstract, utopian, and yet become pantopian or panic, meaning the expansion of this singularity in every place?

Though born left-handed, I write with my right hand, and the happiness of living in a body thus completed has never left me, so that I still beseech schoolmasters not to thwart, as one says today, my companions on the port side, but to give them an immense advantage and to harmonize their bodies by forcing them to hold the pencil in the right, complementary, hand. And, symmetrically, to complete right-handers in the same way. Since most contemporaries abandon the pen for the computer console, their keyboard demands conjugated fingers.

The line that separates the left from the right—and the female from the male—I do not know through where it passes, through the middle of the organism, doubtless as geometric and formal as the frontier or the axis on the river or the straits, but the whole body changes and is transformed depending on whether it turns right or left, hemiplegic in both cases, or whether it agrees to risk going toward the other bank, a hermaphrodite, a ship with two sides, for achievement and agreement. Once again, the third place, rare, invades the system in its entirety: the whole person calls himself right-handed and left-handed—or complete.

Thus the third place is annulled in black memory or dilates in the soul: open, dilated, it is filled with third persons. To learn: to become pregnant with others and oneself. Begetting and crossbreeding. Just as the third person is spirit, the Harlequin's coat and flesh are sown with colored spirits: fires.

A beat, a pulsation, a trembling like the kind one sees in a curtain of flames that shimmers and expands suddenly to illuminate as far as the horizon, yet suddenly can turn in on itself so as to illuminate nothing but a narrow and limited vicinity or to be annulled in darkness, a trembling scintillation, animate, in this book, the discovery, in many regions, of these third places—rare, fine as limits, sharp as crests—singularities that one can say are out of the ordinary, ambidextrous people, hermaphrodites, messengers that belong to two worlds because they put them in communication with each other, like Hermes, the god of translators, flying from one riverbank to another, but who can also be found on earth or in the sea, on islands or paths; these third places give the naked and visible flesh, hot and tangible in life or in the space discernible on a map, of the most intellectual, learned, or cultural project, and of a tolerant ethics, of third-instruction, a harmonious middle/ milieu, a daughter between two banks, of scientific culture and of knowledge culled from the humanities, of expert erudition and of artistic narrative, of the gathered and the invented, conjugated together because in reality the single reason of universal science and of singular suffering cannot be separated. Since today urgency demands it, history recaptures this project, one that was rare not so long ago.

And suddenly, multiple begetting: these singularities, spatial, carnal, pedagogic, without anything having predicted it, are sown everywhere, on the entire body, across the riverbed, in intellectual space, to the point of outlining a synthesis or pointing to a universal. The small flame bursts. From nothing to everything; from the sum total back to zero. From closed communication between two first persons, to the singular or plural, to the whole set of these thirds who are annulled or become all of society, of the universe, of being, and of morality. Never would I have hoped for so much bright light, though, despite its flashes, it tolerates the black shadow, through the incessant divisions of its vibration.

Low, the flame lit up neighborhoods; high, the fire illuminates the world. The pages flame as in a hearth where the dance, long or short, of sparks quickly licks the local, lights up the global, and suddenly returns to darkness: day, night, morning, chiaroscuro. See: the fire lights up; evil: the flame burns. Two foci, at once: sparkling science, searing pain.

Among improbable and difficult circumstances—war, storms, the fortunes and misfortunes of the sea, we reached a nil island lost in the immensity of the Pacific where the natives were given over to strange behaviors, but from whom we learned that the rule always followed by those like us, from the four sides of the water, was reduced to an exception, doubtless monstrous, of a universal only reflected and discovered by chance in this abandoned singularity. As if a bias had conquered the whole volume, while human and reasonable prudence was taking refuge in remote localities.

The oblique has conquered the general. The universal lodges in the singular.

Scintillating flames: a yellow dwarf, the sun lights up not so much the world as a corner of the universe, and the latter does not allow itself to be seen in its majesty except during brief and lightning intuitions, which are obvious and problematic, but nocturnal. The theory of knowledge has never stopped taking the emission or expansion of light as its model. Light pushed back the darkness and was supposed to triumph in space and in history. Having become, recently, relativistic and modest, our contemporaries, henceforth prudent, are fascinated with aiming a luminous, quasi-punctual beam, as fine and pointed as a laser, at details. We have abandoned unitary synthesis to find ourselves or lose ourselves deliciously in the delicacies of the infinitely small, forgetful of the universal in favor of singularities that carry meaning. I willingly admit to having long prefered the exquisitely workable local to the pretentious global, which is always suspected of abuse: and I swam toward the middle of a river or questioned myself gravely about my hands or the islands, attentive to these small, frivolous details.

Defined by closure and specificity, the ideal of knowledge thus passed from general laws to detailed debate, reaching a point of immeasurably disseminated fragmentation. Surprise: in some places or neighborhoods, the universal was lurking. And, renewed astonishment, the universal asks neither to stretch out nor to reign; adamantine, it demands, on the contrary, to be returned to the close and fine locality where it was unearthed. The flame, minis-cule, becomes immense, and returns to ground level.

Irregularly, from the local to the global, this knowledge pulsates, dances, trembles, vibrates, scintillates like a curtain of flames. At the center of the system, the sun lights up the whole; this marginal dwarf just happens to have been thrown there, somewhere in the universe. These two propositions, the universal and the singular, for a single sun, remain true at the same time. Facing the sun and as universal as science, the question of evil and of suffering, of injustice and of hunger, tenebrous, occupies the second focus or the darkness of the universe, as well as the singular existence of the indigent and sorrowful man.

This pulsation touches not only on clear knowledge or on evil, thus on the principles of every apprenticeship and on the span of knowledge—a wisp of straw caressed by a ray of light emanating from a fissure, or a firmament in its entirely under the reign of mid-day, customs, and law—but also on their quality, on their very expression.

Devoted to the search for truth, we do not always reach it; if and when we arrive, through analyses or equations, experiments or formal proofs, but also through experimentation, sometimes, and, when experimentation doesn't get you there, let the story go there, if it can; if meditation fails, why not try narrative? Why would language always remain right-handed or male, hemiplegic and limited to a half? Aristotle said it excellently: "The philosopher, as such, tells a story, as well," but added, "the one who tells a story, in some sense, reveals himself to be a philosopher."

Brought up in irregular flames, instructed, educated, he engenders in himself third persons or spirits that sprinkle his body and his soul with their form and their brightness as much as the pieces and bits compose the colored fires of Harlequin's coat or the white fire that is their summation.

Mind: clear light, modest and restrained, colorfully patterning the body and the soul just as millions of nighttime suns spangle the universe.

Reborn, he knows, he takes pity.
Finally, he can teach.

1980–1990